Britishisms

A Dictionary
of words, idioms, and phrases
characteristic of British English.

compiled and edited
by
Lawrence Holofcener

Published by
Partners Press
Canal Road
Princeton, New Jersey

First Edition
1981
Revised and Expanded Edition
1984

ISBN-0-942676-78-5

Manufacutured in the United States of America

A word from the author

British English is very nearly a foreign language, as most Americans who have visited Great Britain will verify. Proof of this is *Britishisms,* containing almost five thousand words and phrases common to Britons and confoundingly uncommon to us.

Granted, communication gaps are being plugged through radio, television, and jet travel, and many *Britishisms* are seeping into our lexicon, as are Americanisms into theirs. But the average American is struck with the surprising difference between his language and that of the man on the London sidewalk. Apart from accent variants, and these alone can be ear-shattering, the visitor often finds himself at sea in a country he feels should be a second home. He will ask for the nearest gas station and be answered with a frown. She will try to buy potato chips and wind up with french fries. The child wanting cookies or candy will go hungry unless he knows the secret words.

The nice thing, of course, is that when we invited the British out of our country some centuries ago they left behind their language, along with a lot of their countrymen. So there is every reason to believe that, fortified with your *Britishisms,* a soupçon of sign language, and a profusion of smiles, you should easily get along in Great Britain without an interpreter.

England and neighboring Wales, Scotland and Ireland, are not just beautiful, but abounding in tradition and history. Yet quite a few Americans bypass the UK on their first trip abroad, feeling that it's not really and truly a foreign country. To that notion *Britishisms* pipes: That's bletherskite! Crawl out of your Humber saloon, open the boot and drag out your Wellies and anorak. Then onto Shanks' mare for a constitutional up a down or down a wold. Nip into a costermonger's for a fresh-up or natter in the local with a nob. It's a dead cert you'll be as keen as mustard on everything and everyone British, as is

Your most humble servant,

P.S. This enlarged edition is partly due to some good-humored friends and readers who've suggested more than 700 additions. And, too, this edition is being distributed in England as well, for those tourists and visitors who somehow have gone to that foreign place without a dictionary! And who knows, perhaps even some of our British friends may purchase a *Britishisms* for — well, to see how a colonial interprets his language?

Again, for Julia —
my beautiful editor, publisher,
business manager and friend.

Lawrence Holofcener is a playwright, lyricist, actor, director and sculptor. His plays and musicals have been produced in New York, London, Paris, Stockholm and Mexico City, one of which is the musical comedy, "Mr. Wonderful." He has performed on Broadway in "Hello Dolly" and "Stop The World I Want To Get Off," and in numerous regional theaters. His one-man and group sculpture shows have earned him an unusual following both in America and England, and his composite portrait of Laurence Olivier will soon be unveiled at the Chichester Festival Theatre. Mr. Holofcener and his wife Julia are devoted anglophiles. She is currently President of the Princeton Branch of the English-Speaking Union, and he has been lecturing to its branches throughout the Eastern Seaboard.

Contents

Preface

The dictionary is divided into two sections. The first pertains to the traveler's obvious needs; travel, lodging, food, etc. The second contains the complete dictionary.

In the book are many terms which are well-known to us. For brevity's sake, the familiar definitions of these are omitted.

There are quite a number of nautical terms. It should be remembered that the British live on islands, and that no one is more than a hundred miles from the sea. Similarly, the many foreign words are a result of England's proximity to the European continent.

Once the reader is accustomed to the sound of British English, his ear will no doubt become tuned to all sorts of idiomata not contained herein. Therefore at the end of each letter group there is space for his or her own *Britishisms*.

Any suggestions or additions will be gratefully received.

Travel

AA Box emergency telephone booth for Auto. Assoc. members;
  RAC Box for members of Royal Auto. Club.
accommodation road access road.
advance booking reservations.
articulated lorry trailer truck.
bonnet engine hood.
booking hall ticket office.
boot trunk, luggage compartment.
box junction intersection; **box spanner** lug wrench.
bus city bus.
cabrank taxicab line.
caravan travel trailer.
carman van or truck driver.
carriage-way roadway.
car park parking lot, garage.
centre reservation median stripe.
chippings gravel.
circus traffic circle.
city centre downtown.
clearway highway with no stopping allowed.
coach long-distance bus: tour bus; railway car.
coach party tour bus.
coach stop pub, cafe or restaurant accepting buses.
coupe two-door car, usu convertible.
cul-de-sac dead end.
cycle-car three-wheeled car.
day-return (ticket) cheapest round-trip fare.
demister defroster.
Derv diesel fuel.
dipswitch dimming switch.

diversion detour.

dormobile camper car, van.

double-bend S-curve.

drophead convertible.

dual carriageway superhighway.

dynamo generator.

enquiry information.

estate car station wagon.

flat battery dead battery.

flyover overpass.

garage service station.

gearbox transmission; **gear-lever** gearshift.

give way yield.

goods vehicle delivery truck.

guard train conductor.

headlamp headlight.

hire rent.

hire-purchase buy on installment.

hood roof.

hooter car horn.

Imperial gallon British gallon equal to 1.2 American gallons.

kerb curb.

landrover country, farm car, like our jeep.

lay by rest-stop along a highway.

L-driver learning driver.

left luggage baggage, check-room.

level crossing railroad crossing.

Lorry truck.

loose chippings gravel.

lost property lost and found.

metalled surface paved road.

mileometer odometer.

mini type of very small car.

M.O.T. car inspection certificate.

motorist driver.

motorway super-highway, designated M1, M2, etc.

nave wheel hub.

number plate license plate.

oilbox greasebox for brakes.

overtake pass.

paraffin oil kerosene.

pavement sidewalk.

pelican pedestrian-controlled traffic light.

petrol gasoline, rated 2, 3, and 4 star, 2 being regular.

petrol garage service station; gas station.

pull-in roadside cafe; rest stop.

puncture flat tire.

quay pier.

queue up wait in line.

railway railroad; **railway guard** conductor.

return ticket round-trip ticket.

reversing lights back-up lights.

ring road city by-pass road.

roundabout traffic circle, with those already in the circle having the right-of-way.

running-in break-in period of a new car.

running lights parking lights.

saloon sedan, four-door car.

shunt switch.

side lights parking lights.

silencer muffler.

single ticket one-way.

sleeper pullman.

spanner wrench.

sparking plug sparkplug.

speed limits unless indicated, 60 mph on highways, 70 on the motorways. Many motorists travel over 100 on the motorways, illegally and dangerously. Travelers are wise to keep to the posted limits esp with the confusion of keeping to left.

straight on straight ahead.

subway pedestrian passage beneath a road or railroad.

sump crankcase.

T-junction T.

tail-lamp tail light.

tarred road macadam, paved road.

top it up fill it up (gas tank).

torch flashlight.

track-up wheel alignment.

tube, underground subway.

turnpike road toll road.

underground subway.

van panel, delivery truck.

verge highway shoulder.

way-in entrance.

way-out exit.

windscreen windshield.

wing fender.

wireless radio.

zebra crossing pedestrian crossing.

Food & Restaurants

afternoon tea from a tea break to light lunch, served 3-5 p.m., but usually tea, scones, cookies.

aubergines eggplant.

B & B bed and breakfast, meaning a clean comfortable room in a farm or country, or town house, without bath, and with an English breakfast; juice, eggs, bacon, sausage, tomato and plenty of toast and coffee.

bangers sausages.

bap hamburger roll.

beetroot beets.

bill check.

bill of fare menu.

biscuits, dry crackers, usually for cheese.

biscuits, sweet cookies.

booking reserving ahead.

broad bean lima bean.

bubble & squeak potatoes and cabbage.

buns dinner rolls.

butter bean lima bean.

cakes cookies.

candy floss cotton candy.

champers champagne.

char familiar word for tea, after char-woman's tea.

charger large flat serving dish.

charlotte pudding with apples or other fruit, breadcrumbs.

chicory endive.

chips french fries.

chipolata slim-jim.

chip shop fish & chips take-out shop.

chocolates candy bars.

cockaleeky Scottish soup made with leeks.

coffee bar shop or cafe serving tea, coffee, cakes and light sandwiches.

cockle edible small shell-fish; snail.

cole kind of cabbage.

comfit candied fruit.

conserve candied fruit or jam.

container tin can.

cooker stove.

corn grain.

cornet ice-cream cone.

Cornish cream thick, almost, sour whipped cream, served with tea.

Cornish pasty small, covered, meat pot-pie.

Cornish wafer cookie.

costermonger fruit and vegetable stall or store.

cottage pie chopped meat, mashed potatoes baked in a pie shell.

courgettes zucchini; squash.

demarara raw sugar.

devil highly season food.

Devon cream thick, clotted cream served with tea & scones.

digestive biscuits wholemeal cookies.

double-cream whipping cream.

elevenses morning coffee or tea break.

eggflip eggnog.

engaged occupied (esp the lavatory).

farce stuffing.

fillet steak boneless sirloin.

finnan haddie smoked haddock.

finnoc trout.

fish & chips deep-fried fish, occasionally flounder, and larger french fries, sold in chip shops to go. Buy only at frying times, posted on the door. Usually doused with vinegar.

fishmonger fish store.

fishpaste sandwich spread made of fish.

flan upside-down cake; fruit and sponge-cake, fruit tart.

Lodging

accommodation lodging, room.

account hotel bill.

advance booking reservation.

all-found all expenses included.

baggage luggage.

bed & breakfast country, farm, or town house accommodations, providing a clean, comfortable room without private bath, and a great English breakfast, perhaps the best bargain in the country. Often found in pubs as well.

booking reservations (see TIC).

box-room luggage room.

calor-gas bottled gas.

chamber room.

commissionaire doorman, door-keeper.

concierge in better old hotels esp a clerk who books theater tickets, tours, rail, bus, plane reservations, etc. An in-house travel agent.

cot crib.

duvet down quilt.

first floor second floor, usu where restaurants, meeting rooms are located.

fitted built-in; **fitted carpet** wall-to-wall.

full board 3 meals.

ground floor first floor, lobby.

hire car rental car.

lift elevator.

lift-boy elevator boy, bell-hop.

lounge usu sitting room with stuffed furniture; lobby.

lounge bar better furnishings than the public bar.

mains service electricity.

maisonette large apartment, half-house.

moving-staircase escalator.

porter doorman, bell-hop.

purpose-built new, not renovated.

railway hotel hotel close to stations, usu flea-bags.

reception hotel from desk.

receptionist desk clerk.

self-contained room or flat with cooking facilities.

taxi gotten by the porter, can be phoned for in most cities.

TIC Tourist Information Center; dotted around the country, they provide information and reservations, known as 'Book-a-bed-Ahead.'

Pubs, Wine & Spirits

foie gras pate.

full-round whole sandwich.

frangipane almond-flavored pastry.

frenchbean stringbean.

fruiterer fruit market; stall.

fry-up mixed foods fried together.

gateau fancy cake.

gherkin pickle, usu sweet.

ginger-pop giner-beer, ale.

greengrocer fruit & vegetable stall, market.

griskin lean bacon, rinds.

haggis Scottish dish of sheep innards and oatmeal, seasoned and boiled in the sheep's stomach ining. Quite tasty, despite the sound of the ingredients.

high tea usu a light supper, esp in the North served at 5.

ice lollies popsicles.

ices ice cream, cones.

Irish stew stew usu made of mutton, lamb, and potatoes.

jaffa large orange from Israel.

jam jelly; **jampot** jar.

jelly jello.

joint a roast of meat.

julienne clear broth with finely chopped vegetables.

kickshaw elaborately prepared dish.

lady's fingers okra.

lobscouse meat and vegetable stew.

maize corn, usu off the cob.

marrow squash.

minced chopped, ground, usu meat; hamburger.

10

mincepie meat pie.
monkey nut peanut.
mousse frozen cream and gelatin dessert.
napkin cloth napkin.
parboil to boil.
parson's nose rump of cooked chicken.
partridge small British gamebird.
patty small pot-pie.
pease peas.
pip fruit pit; seed.
plaice N. sea fish.
ploughman's lunch cheese, bread, pickle & onion.
plumcake raisin-cake.
porkpie small pie with chopped pork, etc.
prawns large shrimp.
pub lunch hot meal served in some pubs; usu good value and taste,
    worth a detour from the motorways.
pudding boiled or baked mixture of flour & suet, etc.
puff-paste light pastry; napoleon.
push-basket shopping cart.
queen cake small raisin bun.
roasting jack broiling spit; rotisserie.
rock dogfish.
rump steak cheaper sirloin steak than fillet.
runner beans french beans.
salad generally a meat or cheese plate garnished with lettuce.
salad cream mayonnaise.
sally-lunn hot buttered tea cake.
salmagundi chopped meat seasoned with anchovies, etc.
salmon trout sea-trout.
salf-beef corned beef.
salt cellar salt shaker.
sand-glass egg-timer.
saucepan small pot.
savoy winter cabbage.

scampi large fried shrimp.

scone raisin bun.

semolina cream of wheat.

serve to wait on.

serviette napkin.

shepherd's pie meat, onions, mashed potatoes in a pie.

shortcake shortbread.

sippet toast or fried bread used as a garnish.

skilly thin broth or stew.

smorbrod Danish appetizers served cold.

sorbet sherbet, ices.

souse pickle.

spend a penny use the bathroom, toilet.

sprat small tasty fish.

squash drink made of fruit syrup and water.

stick-jaw taffy; bubble-gum.

sultanas raisins.

swede yellow turnip.

sweet dessert.

sweeting eating apple.

sweetmeat chocolate candy.

sweet oil olive oil; salad oil.

sweets candy.

sweet-shop candy store.

Swiss roll jelly roll.

take-away to go, take-out.

tart piece of or small pie.

tea English tea is usu from India in flakes, served in a pot which
   is first heated, very strong, and poured into a cup which has milk
   in the bottom. Traditionally, it is served on rising, with all meals,
   and in the afternoon. Most hotels serve excellent teas, esp old ones
   in London.

tinned canned; from tin cans.

toffy taffy.

treacle molasses.

12

trifle fruit shortcake, cream — anything but a trifle.
tuckshop candy store near a school.
tunny tunafish.
turbot flat fish similar to flounder.
vacant empty, unoccupied.
veg vegetable.
vinaigrette vinegar bottle, jar.
w.c. water-closet; bathroom with toilet.
whelk edible shellfish like a conch.
whitebait sprats or minnows eaten as delicacy.
Worcester Sauce Worcestershire sauce.
Yorkshire pudding light pudding baked in beef fat.

Clothing

anorak hooded jacket; parka.
bespoke tailor made-to-measure men's clothing store.
billfold wallet.
bowler derby hat.
braces men's suspenders.
briefs jockey shorts.
brogues heavy walking shoes.
brolly umbrella.
bumbershoot umbrella.
carpet-slippers slippers.
cat-suit woman's jumpsuit.
clothes peg clothespin.
coney rabbit fur.
court shoe pump.
covert-coat man's short overcoat.
cravat necktie.
deerstalker Sherlock Holmes hat, with flaps.
DJ dinner jacket.
dinner suit tuxedo.
dollar bag soft handbag with strings.
drawers undershorts.
dressing-case traveling case with toilet articles.
dressing-gown bathrobe.
fancy work embroidery.
flat iron iron.
fob pocket in vest for watch.
galluses suspenders.
gym shoes sneakers.
haberdasher store selling ribbons, thread, notions.
hair-laquer hair spray.

hairslide barrette.
handbag lady's pocketbook.
henna hair-dye or rinse.
hosiery men's underwear, socks, ties.
jerkin man's leather vest.
jersey sweater.
jumper lady's sweater.
kirby grip bobbie pin.
knickerbockers knickers.
knickers ladies underpants.
lace-ups shoes or boots fastened by laces.
lounge suit business suit.
mackintosh raincoat.
nail varnish nail polish.
nappie diaper.
Norfolk jacket man's jacket with pleats and belt.
note case wallet.
outfitter clothing store.
outsize extra-large.
overshoes rubbers, galoshes.
pants undershorts.
plimsolls sneakers.
plus fours knickers.
pocketbook wallet.
press stud snap.
purse woman's change purse.
reach-me-downs ready-to-wear clothes.
reefer short thick double-breasted coat.
rollneck turtle-neck.
sabot wood-soled shoe.
sark night-shirt.
setting lotion hair-spray.
singlet man's undershirt.
sleevelink cufflink, stud.
slipper woman's evening shoe.

smalls man's undershirt.
spencer short wool jacket.
suiting material for suit or coat.
sunshade parasol.
suspenders woman's garters.
swanskin flannel.
swim-suit bathing suit.
tailor men's clothing store.
tights panty hose.
trews tartan trousers.
trilby man's soft felt hat.
trousers pants.
turn-ups cuffs (pants).
vanity bag lady's handbag for cosmetics.
vest man's undershirt.
waistcoat man's vest.
windcheater windbreaker.
winklepickers shoes with pointed toes.
woolly sweater.
zip-fastener zipper.

Sports & Games

ace skilled sportsman.

address (golf) take aim and stance.

air cushion air mattress.

airgun bb gun.

alley white, large marble (shooter).

angler fisherman.

Ashes, The fictional trophy of cricket Test Matches.

Association Football professional soccer.

autodrome car race-track.

bat cricket-bat; ping-pong paddle.

bathe swim.

bomb. success.

bowls game played with biased wooden balls, on a bowling green.

British Open (golf) at St. Andrews, Scotland.

bumble-puppy game with tennis ball tied to a post.

catapult sling-shot.

changing room locker-room.

clasp-knife pocket-knife.

course race-track.

crackers fire crackers.

cup-tie soccer competition, much like our World Series.

curling game of skidding flat heavy stones over ice.

Derby annual horse-race at Epsom Downs.

dinghy small sailboat.

draughts checkers.

draw tie.

links golf course.

meet gathering of huntsmen and hounds.

niblick pitching wedge.

pack deck (of cards).

pirn fishing reel.
pitch playing field.
punter horse bettor.
pushball game played with 6 ft. ball.
rowing boat rowboat.
solo two-handed whist.
spillikins pick-up-sticks.
squails tiddly-winks.
tenpins bowling.
torpid racing scull.
try touchdown (cricket).
walkaway easy win.
Wimbledon British Open tennis championships, early July.
whist card game for four players, early form of bridge.

Theater

advance booking reservation.

attendant usher.

balcony rows of seats above the mezzanine, below the gallery.

cinema movie; movie theater.

dress circle first mezzanine.

film movie.

first night opening night.

gallery second balcony; highest, cheapest seats.

gangway aisle.

gods cheapest, highest seats.

interval intermission.

lift elevator.

mezzanine floor just below stage.

queue to wait in line.

stalls orchestra.

tea once a custom in London theaters, now only occasionally observed, of serving tea and cookies at your seat during the intermission. Must be reserved with the ushers.

upper circle second mezzanine of first balcony.

West End reference to London theater district.

Advice to Tourists

Driving Tips

Remember to keep to the left-hand side of the road! Especially after a roundabout. Practice looking to the right at a junction or T. Stay to the left lanes on motorways unless you plan to drive at speeds exceeding seventy (the legal limit, though it is common to find cars going a hundred and more!). Watch for bicycles; they are more prevalent in England. Check your windshield wipers; it is likely as not to rain every day. Don't keep driving on Empty while searching for a lower price for petrol. Excepting London and holiday areas the price of a gallon is generally the same and staggeringly high.

Refreshments

Many roadside and village pubs serve good lunches; sandwiches, soups, buffets and hot meals at reasonable prices. Beer is served in pints and halves. While "best bitter" is traditional, lager is similar to American beer. Hours for lunch are strictly between 12 and 2:30, but they are extended in hotels and restaurants.

Fish & Chip shops, take-out only, are to be found in most towns. Warning: buy only at frying hours and at places popular with the locals.

Teas are served in pubs, restaurants, hotels and country houses and consist of tea with milk, sandwiches, cookies or cake. Cream tea is with scones (biscuits), thick cream and jam. Tea time is between 3 and 5 in the afternoon.

Accommodations

Hotels can be found in nearly every town and many villages, from modern to ancient, with only one consistency; high tariff. The purse-minders should heed the B & B signs. It usually means a large comfortable clean room without bath, and a great breakfast consisting of juice, eggs, bacon, sausage, fried tomatoes, and plenty of toast and coffee.

"Railway Hotels" are the closest thing to our "flea-bags," and should be avoided.

Pubs often offer excellent accommodation at B & B rates.

Guide to Abbreviations

abbr	abbreviation	*n*	noun
adv	adverb	N	North
adj	adjective	NE	North-East
Aust	Australian	*naut*	nautical
coll	colloquial	*pt*	past tense
conj	conjunction	*pl*	plural
dial	dialect	*pref*	prefix
E	East	*prep*	preposition
esp	especially	*pron*	pronoun
etc	etcetera	S	South
exclam	exclamation	SE	South-East
euph	euphemism	SW	South-West
expl	expletive	*Scots*	Scottish
fig	figurative(ly)	*sl*	slang
Fr	French	*theat*	theatrical
Germ	German	*tr*	trademark
interj	interjection	usu	usually
Ir	Irish	*v*	verb
Ital	Italian	*vulg*	vulgar
leg	legal	*Wel*	Welsh
mil	military		

A

abattoir *n Fr* slaughter-house.

abed *adv* in bed, confined to bed.

abigail *n coll* lady's maid.

about *adv* close at hand; **up and about** out of bed.

aboveboard *adv, adj* without concealment; fair, honorable.

above oneself conceited, elated.

abroad *adv* overseas; in a foreign land; away from one's home; wide of the truth; **going abroad** traveling overseas, probably to Europe.

absquatulate *v coll* run away.

accommodation road access road.

accommodations *n* rooms, lodgings; housing.

according to Cocker quite correct.

account *n* hotel bill; **of some account** held in esteem; **call to account** demand an explanation from.

acolyte *n* follower, assistant.

accursed *adj* under a curse; detestable.

ace *n* extremely skilled sportsman, marksman; **within an ace of** a hair's breadth.

acid drop sourball.

across, come meet by accident; **put it across** get even with, impose upon.

act a part behave hypocritically, ridiculously.

act of grace formal pardon granted by Act of Parliament.

actionable *adj.* liable; grounds for suit.

actual, the money; cash.

acushla *n Ir* darling.

adder *n* adding-machine.

address *v* apply oneself (to some activity); **address the ball** (in golf) take aim and stance.

adit *n* entrance, approach.

admin *adj coll* administrative, administration.

admiralty *n* office of an admiral; board of commissioners which oversees the navy; building where the board meets.

ado *n* doing, action; fuss; bustle; trouble; **with much ado** with much difficulty.

adust *adj* scorched, parched.

advance *n* raise in pay; rise in price.

advance booking reservation.

advancement *n* promotion.

advert *n* advertisement.

advisement *n* consultation.

aerial *n* antenna.

afar *adv* far away; at a distance.

afoot *adv, adj* active, moving; **something's afoot** something's wrong.

afternoon farmer lazy fellow.

afternoonified *adj sl* swanky; putting on airs.

afters *n coll* dessert; **any afters?**

aga *n* popular, expensive kitchen stove fueled by oil or coal, found in many farm and country houses.

age-long *adj* lasting a long period.

aggro *n sl* deliberate aggressive violence usu by gang.

agley *adv Scots* awry, badly.

aglimmer *adv* glimmering.

agnail *n* torn cuticle.

agog *adj, adv* in excited expectation.

agony-bags *n sl* bag pipes.

agrestic *adj* rural, rustic.

ah *exclam* you don't say! I quite agree; oh yes; I see; settled!

aide-de-camp *n* officer who assists a general.

aim high be ambitious.

air-cushion *n* air mattress.

airdrome *n* airport.

airer *n* clothes drying rack.

air, give one the fire; dismiss.

airgun *n* b-b gun.

air-hostess *n* stewardess.

airing cupboard clothes-warming closet (usu containing heater).

air, in the current vogue, rumor.

airs and graces affected mannerisms.

airscrew *n* propeller.

airship *n* dirigible, blimp.

airy-fairy *adj coll* fanciful, whimsical; too delicate, impractical, vague.

akimbo *adv* with hands on hips and elbows jutting out.

alarms and excursions fuss; petty quarrels.

alarmist *n* one who raises unnecessary alarm; fear-monger.

albert *n* man's watch-chain.

alderman *n* member of borough or county council; councilman.

Alderney *n* breed of cattle.

alehouse *n* pub.

'alf a mo' bristly, short moustache.

alienist *n* psychiatrist.

All Fool's Day *n* April Fool's Day.

all-a-cock messed up; fouled up; **all brandy** first class; **all found** complete; everything included; **all his buttons on** alert, quick; **all-in** exhausted; the works; no holds barred; **all jaw** more noise than work; **all my eye** nonsense; **all over grumble** inferior; **all overish** edgy, nervous; **all over oneself** self-pleased, over-confident; **all poshed up** smartly dressed; **all-rounder** one excelling at many sports, things; **all smoke, gammon and pickles** nonsense; worthless; **all up with** ruined, done-for.

allsorts *n* licorice candies, among others.

ally, alley *n* large white marble used in playing marbles (the shooter).

almsbox *n* church donation or charity box.

almshouse *n* house endowed by charity for the poor and aged.

Alsation *n* police dog; german shepherds.

altar boy acolyte, follower.

altogether, the in the nude.

aluminum *n* aluminum.

amah *n* Indian wet-nurse; English child's Indian nurse.

amenities *n* conveniences; comforts; personal items; advantages.

American cloth type of oil cloth.

Americanism *n* any peculiarity of idiom, accent, vocabulary, characteristic of the United States.

amongst *prep* among.

anchoret *n* religious recluse, hermit.

angler *n* fisherman, esp fly-fishing, river-fishing.

Anglican *n* member of the Church of England.

ankle-biters *n sl* tightly-cuffed pants.

anklet *n* ornamental chain worn about the ankle.

Anne's fan thumb to nose and fingers outspread.

annual *n sl* one's yearly vacation.

anorak *n* parka; windbreaker.

answerable *adj* responsible.

ant-heap *n* ant-hill.

antic *adj* like a clown, buffoon; grotesque.

anti-clockwise *adj, adv* counter-clockwise.

anybody's guess a matter of uncertainty.

any more for any more? second helping, anyone?

apeak *adv. adj naut* vertical.

appalling *adj* shocking, horrible.

apparel *n* clothing, dress.

apple of discord cause of dispute.

apple-pie bed bed made for a joke with sheets so turned it cannot be entered; short-sheeted.

apple-pie order neat condition.

apple and pears, up the *sl* (cockney) up the stairs.

appointments equipment, furnishings, decorations.

approachable *adj* friendly, welcoming.

arab, street arab young vagrant, rogue; sly merchant.

arcade *n* covered avenue of shops; shopping mall.

arf a tick *sl* wait a minute; in a minute.

argil (arjil) *n* potter's clay.

argot (argo) *n* thieves' slang: slang of a particular class.

argue the leg off an iron pot quarrelsome.

argus-eyed *adj* extremely vigilant.

argy-bargy *n coll* dispute, argument.

arise out of be a consequence, cause of.

ark of refuge bolt-hole; safety house.

armiger *n* esquire; person entitled to heraldic arms.

army-list *n* official list of Army officers.

arras *n* tapestry for walls.

arriswise *adv* diagonally; forming ridges.

'Arry & 'Arriet *sl* costermonger and his lady partner.

arse (ahss) *n vulg* buttocks; *naut* stern; **arse about** *v vulg* play around.

arse, ask my I don't know; **arse over tit, turkey** head over heels.

Arthurian *adj* pertaining to legends, etc of King Arthur.

article, the (very) exactly the right thing, person.

articulated lorry trailer truck.

art-silk *n* rayon.

Ashes, the fictitious trophy of the Test Matches (cricket) between England and Australia.

ashbin *n* trashcan, garbage can.

ashpan *n* pan to collect ashes beneath a grate.

ass *n coll* jerk, fool.

assize *n* trial by judge and jury; periodic sessions held by judges in provincial centers throughout England.

Association Football professional soccer.

assurance society insurance company.

astraddle *adv.* astride.

atelier (atelyay) *n Fr* artist's studio.

attache-case *n* briefcase.

attendant *n* usher.

aubergine *n* egg-plant.

auburn *adj* reddish brown.

auger *n* drill-bit.

Aunt Sally easy set-up.

au pair (opair) young person, usu foreign, who cares for children, in exchange for room, board and pocket money.

Aussie *n coll* Australian.

autoclave *n* pressure-cooker.

autocue *n* teleprompter.
autocycle *n* motorbike.
autodrome *n* care racetrack.
autumn *n* Fall.
avast *interf naut* stop, cease!
avenue *n* driveway to house bordered by rows of trees.
aviator *n* pilot.
awfully *adv coll* very, extremely
awkward customer possibly dangerous person.
axe-helve *n* axe-handle.

B

baby minder *n* a woman paid to look after babies in her home while the mother is at work; baby-sitter.

Backs *n* lawns and grounds of Cambridge colleges overlooking the river.

backbench *n* any bench in the House of Commons occupied by members who are not Ministers of leading members of the Opposition. **backbenchers.**

backchat *n* impertinent retort; comedians' patter; **backcloth** *n* back-drop in a theater; **backdoor** *adj* secretive, underhand; **back-end** *n* rear end; last part; end of Autumn; **back-handed** *adj* underhanded, unfair; **back-number** *n* earlier issue of magazine or newspaper; out-of-date thing or person; **backset** *n* setback, reversal, release; **backsheet** *n* last page of a newspaper; **backstairs** *n* servants' staircase; *adj* underhand, secret.

back up, get one's become angry.

bad form *adv sl* ill-mannered, incorrect behavior.

baddish *adj* slightly irreputable.

baggage *n* luggage; common or worthless person, things.

bagman *n coll* salesman; tramp.

bags *adj* plenty.

bailie *n Scots* an alderman.

bairn *n* a child.

baize *n* coarse woolen material.

balderdash *n* jumble of meaningless words; nonsense!

ballard-monger *n* music seller, publisher; an inferior poet.

ballocks *n vulg* mix-up; nonsense.

balls-up *n vulg sl* blunder, mistake; mess, confusion.

bally *euph* bloody; **bally-well** certainly.

bandy *v* toss, hit; exchange.

banger *n coll* sausage; noisy old car; hearty kiss.

bang-off at once; **bang-on, bang-up** first class; right on.

bangers & train smash *sl* sausages and tomatoes.

Bank *n* section of The City of London around The Bank Of England.

Bank Holiday *n* day observed as public holiday.

banknote *n* paper money.

banting *n* dieting by avoiding fats, starch and sugar.

bap *n* hamburger bun.

bar *prep* except for, save; **be called to the bar** become a barrister.

Bard *n* Shakespeare; poet who has won the prize at the Welsh Eisteddfod.

bargee *n* barge-worker; **swear like a bargee** swear loudly.

barmaid *n* waitress; **barman** *n* bartender.

barmy *adv* witless, insane, silly.

barney *n sl* fight, brawl.

baronet *n* lowest hereditary title ranking below a baron and above a knight.

barrack *v* jeer, deride.

barrel-organ *n* hurdy-gurdy, organ grinder.

barrister *n* member of the legal profession with the right to plead as advocate in superior courts.

barrow *n* burial mound; wheel-barrow; push-cart; **barrow-boy** *n* fruit-seller's helper.

bash *v* strike, beat violently; **have a bash** take a chance, make an attempt.

bat *n* cricket bat; ping-pong paddle.

bath *n* bathtub; **go to Bath** get going, be off.

bathe *v* swim; **bathing-gear** *n* swimwear.

bathing-machine *n* hut on wheels taken into the sea.

batman *n* servant.

bawdy-house *n* brothel.

B.B.C. *n* British Broadcasting Corporation; non-commercial radio and television.

beadle *n* porter at a college lodge; servant.

beak *n sl* policeman; judge; teacher.

beam ends, be on one's in a bad way, poorly.

eard v approach boldly, defy.

earskin n tall furry headgear worn by the Brigade of Guards.

ed-sitter n one room apartment.

edstead n headboard of a bed; bed frame.

eeb, the *abbr coll* B.B.C.

eefeater n Yeoman of the Guard; caretaker of the Tower of London.

eer and skittles, not all not easy.

eerocracy n *coll* brewers, publicans.

eeton, Mrs. old cookbook like The Settlement.

eetroot n beets.

eezer n *sl* nose; fellow.

eggarly *adj* poor, valueless.

ehest n command.

ehonkey n *coll* buttocks.

ellpull n church bell-rope; **bell-wether** n leading sheep; leader.

elt v speed; **belt up** shut up.

ender n pair of pliers.

enedick n newly married man.

ent *adj* crooked, dishonest.

enzine n inflammable liquid cleaner.

erk n *sl* stupid person.

erlin wool n coarse wool for knitting or embroidery.

espoke *adv* made-to-order clothing.

espoke tailor men's custom made haberdasher.

etween-whiles in the meantime.

etwixt *prep* between.

everage n soft-drink, soda; drink.

iddy n *coll* unpleasant old woman; hag.

iffin n variety of red cooking apple.

ig dipper *coll* roller coaster.

ight n curve, bend; curve of a river; shallow bay.

ilge n nonsense.

ill n restaurant check; **billfold** n wallet; **bill-of-fare** n menu.

illingsgate n coarse, vulgar language.

illycock n *coll* bowler hat.

bin container, basket, bucket, for bread, coal, corn-meal, etc.

bind over put on probation.

bird *n sl* attractive girl; **bird-lime** *sl* droppings.

Biro *n* ballpoint pen.

biscuit, dry cracker, esp for cheese; **biscuit, sweet** cookie; **take the biscuit** take the best.

bit *n* small coin; tiny piece of something; **bit of all right** nice going; I like that.

bitch, to mess up, spoil.

bitter *n* ordinary draft beer (English).

bits *n* pieces; **take it to bits** tear it down; take it apart.

black *adj* gloomy, dismal; *v* blacklist; **black maria** paddy-wagon; **black mood** angry; **black pudding** sausage made from pig's blood; **black tie** tuxedo; **black ice** invisible road-ice; **blackcurrant** *n* blackberry; **blackguard** *n* scoundrel; **blackstrap** *n* cheap port wine.

blancmange *n* (blah-mohnge) gelatin-like pudding.

blast *v* use profanity; **blast!** darn it.

blather *n* foolish talk.

blazer *n* solid color sport jacket, usu with school or club emblem on top pocket; uniform for public (private) school boys.

bleeder *n coll* fellow.

bleeding *adj sl* bloody; damned.

bletherskite *n* foolish jabber.

blighter *n sl* contemptible person, a cad.

blighty *n* England; home.

blimey *interj sl* exclamation of surprise.

blimp *n* pompous, ultra-conservative.

blind *n* window shade.

blinking *expl* confounded; darned.

bloater *n* smoked herring.

block of flats apartment house.

bloke *n coll* chap, fellow.

bloomer *n coll* blunder.

bloody *expl* damn! **bloody-minded** *adj* obstinate.

32

blood sports *n* hunting and killing of animals.

blooming *adj coll* wretched, bloody, confounding.

blotto *adj sl* drunk.

blowcock *n* tap on a boiler for releasing steam.

blowed, I'm *expl* blow me down!

blowlamp *n* gas or oil burner for melting solder.

blue *n* player from Oxford or Cambridge Universities; *coll* go on a spending spree.

Blue Peter *n* flag hoisted on ship before sailing.

blue-book *n* document of Parliament or the Privy Council; **bluebottle** *n* policeman; **bluejacket** *n* naval seaman.

blunderbuss *n* short shotgun able to fire many bullets; a clumsy person.

bo *exclam* (utter to startle) **can't say bo to a goose** be very timid.

boaster *n* mason's chisel.

boater *n* straw hat.

boat-train *n* railway train scheduled to meet steamship.

bob or two very rich.

bobby *n* policeman.

Bob's your uncle done! perfect.

bod *n coll* person, fellow.

bodkin *n* blunt needle with large eye.

body-servant *n* valet.

boffin *n sl* scientist.

boiled shirt *n coll* dress shirt with starched collar; snob.

boilersuit *n* overalls.

boko *n sl* nose.

bollocks *n vulg* testicles; nonsense; foul-up.

bolshie *n adj coll* bolshevik, communist, left-wing.

bolt *v* dash away; **bolthole** *n* hiding or safe place; **bolt-upright** *adv* erect in posture.

bomb *n* success; **make a bomb** *coll* be a great success.

bone-idle *adj* extremely lazy.

bone, near the, close to the raw, raunchy; x-rated.

bonkers *adj coll* crazy.

bonnet *n* engine hood.

bonny *adj* pretty, good-looking.

boobyhatch *n naut* covered entrance.

boodle *n sl* crowd; counterfeit money; money; a card-game.

book *v* reverse a seat in advance.

booking clerk *n* box-office clerk.

booking office *n* box-office.

bookplate *n* decorative label inside the cover of a book to indicate the owner.

bookshop *n* book store.

bookstall *n* newspaper stand, store.

boot *n* trunk of a car, luggage compartment.

boot sale rummage sale from car-trunks.

booted *adj* wearing boots.

bootjack *n* device for pulling off boots.

boozer *n coll* drunkard; a public house, a bar.

booze-up *n coll* drinking party.

Borstall *adj* system of reform schools for boys.

bosh *n* nonsense.

bosky *adj* covered with undergrowth, bushy.

boss *n* the knob of a shield, a knob-shaped decoration.

boss-eyed *adj* having a squint; cross-eyed; shady, crooked; **boss-shot** *n* bungled attempt.

bother! *exclam* confound it!

botheration *n* annoyance, irritation; confound it!

bottom *n* last; end (of road); **bottom-drawer** *n coll* hope chest; **bottommost** *adj* lowest.

bought it *coll* got killed.

bouncer *n* bully, cocksure liar; a bare-faced lie.

bound *adj* compelled, obliged.

bounden duty duty to which one is morally bound.

bounder *n coll* ill-bred man with plenty of noisy self-confidence.

Bovril *n tr* a kind of meat extract.

bovver *n sl* bother.

Bow Bells the bells of the church of St Mary-le-bow in Cheapside; **within the sound of Bow Bells** in the City of London.

bowdlerize *v* expurgate (a book) by removing, altering what is considered indelicate or coarse.

bowery *adj* leafy, shady.

bowler *n* cricket player who delivers the ball to the batsman; black derby hat; once part of "uniform" for businessmen.

bowling-green *n* level lawn of smooth turf upon which the game of bowls is played.

bowls *n* game played biased wooden balls on a lawn.

bowser *n* hose for fueling car, aircraft with gasoline; oil tanker.

bow-window *n* bay window; large belly.

box *n* horse's stall in stable or truck, trailer; *v* put in compartment or crate; **box about** *naut* cruise up and down; **box up** *sl* bungle; **boxboard** *n* thick compressed paper, cardboard; **boxcloth** *n* stout closely-woven cloth.

Boxing-day *n* first weekday after Christmas Day, on which presents are usually exchanged or given.

box-junction *n* four-way stop; T junction.

boxroom *n* small room used for storage in attic or cellar; **box-spanner** wrench for removing nuts from car wheel; **box-tree** *n* evergreen or shrub; **box-up** *n* *sl* confusion, bungle.

boxy *adj* small and enclosed.

braces *n* suspenders.

bracing *adv* refreshing.

brad *n* cut nail with square edges.

Brahmin *n* *fig* intellectual, elitist.

braiding *n* embroidery.

brain-fag *n* nervous exhaustion.

brainless *adj* very stupid.

brandysnap *n* crisp kind of gingerbread.

branpie, brantub *n* tub filled with bran into which children dip their hands for hidden prizes.

brash *n* rubble, hedge-clippings.

brass hat *n* *coll* high ranking military officer, the "brass."

brass off grumble.

braw *adj Scots* splendidly dressed, first-rate, pretty.

brawn *n* meat cooked, seasoned and pressed into a mold.

brazier *n* cast iron basket for holding coals or wood; grate.

breach of the peace *leg* public disturbance, riot.

break school recess.

bream *n* freshwater carp.

breastsummer, bressummer *n* beam or lintel over window or door.

breeches (brichiz) *n* trousers, pants.

breeches-buoy *n* lifejacket with inflatable pants.

breeks *n Scots* trousers, pants.

brewster *n* brewer; **Brewster Sessions** *n* time that judges review liquor licenses.

brick *n coll* decent chap, person; **drop a brick** a faux pas, indiscretion.

bridge roll hot dog roll.

brigadier *n mil* commander of a brigade; a brigadier general.

bring to book call to account.

Bristol-board *n* a good artists' cardboard; **Bristol fashion** *adj naut* attaining perfection in appearance and efficiency.

Britannia metal *n* alloy of tin, antimony & copper, often mistaken for pewter.

Britishism *n* a word, idiom, or phrase, etc. characteristic of British English.

British Thermal Unit, BTU heat required to raise temperature of one pound of water one degree F.

British Warm short military overcoat.

broach *n* tool for making holes; awl, boring bit; masonry chisel; spit for roasting; a squinch arch.

broad beans *n* lima beans.

broadsheet *n* large sheet of paper printed only on one side; a ballad or pop music folio; sheet-music.

broadways *adv* along the breadth, laterally.

Brobdingnagian (brobdingnagian) *adj* huge.

brogue *n* stout shoe designed for walking; broad accent, esp Irish.

brolly *n coll* umbrella; **brolly pot** umbrella-stand.

brooch (brOch) *n* pin jewelry.

brougham (broom) *n* four-wheeled closed carriage.

browned-off *sl* thoroughly disgruntled.

brumal *adj* wintry; **brumous** *adj* wintry; foggy.

bub *n sl* woman's breast.

bubble *n fig* anything unsound or speculative; **bubble & squeak** potatoes and cabbage.

bubbly *n sl* champagne.

bucketshop *n* stockbroker not a member of the Exchange who deals in highly speculative or worthless shares.

Buck House *coll* Buckingham Palace, home of British monarchy.

budgie *n* budgerigar; parakeet.

buffet *n* place, table, bar where refreshments are sold.

C

cabbage *n fig* dull, stupid, unimaginative person.

cablese *n coll* jargon of contracted words joined to reduce the cost of telegrams and cables.

caboose *n* oven for cooking outdoors.

cabrank *n* line of taxicabs.

cack-handed *adj* left-handed; clumsy, awkward.

cad *n* ill-bred fellow of mean behavior.

caddy *n* box for holding tea.

cadge *v* get by begging, sponging on others.

cafe (kafay) *n* coffee-house, small restaurant.

cairn *n* heap of stones, esp when raised as a landmark or memorial; breed of small shaggy coated Scots terrier.

cairngorm *n* precious stone found in Scotland.

cake *n* cookie.

cakes and ale fun and merry-making.

Caledonian *n adj* native of Scotland.

calfdozer *n* a small bulldozer.

calkins *n* small, turned-down ends of horse shoes.

call at stop at; **call in** withdraw from circulation; **call out** challenge to a duel; order soldiers into the field; **call up** summon to join armed forces.

callbox *n* public telephone booth; **callboy** *n theat* boy who calls actors to the stage.

calling *n* occupation, business, profession.

calor gas bottled gas.

cambist *n* dealer in bills of exchange.

Cambrian *adj* pertaining to Wales.

camera, in closed court-session.

camion *n* a low wagon, dray; motor trucks.

camisole *n* woman's cotton or linen under-garment.

ampaigner *n* veteran soldier.

anard *n* a false report or hoax.

andyfloss *n* cotton candy.

aning *n* punishing by a cane.

annibis *n* preparation of Indian hemp smoked as an intoxicant drug; hashish, marijuana.

annikan *n* small can; drinking vessel.

annon-fodder *n* soldiers callously sent to their deaths.

anonist *n* expert in canon or church law.

anoodle *v sl* cuddle, caress.

anteen *n* food shop or refreshment counter; case to hold silver or plated flat-ware.

antrip *n Scots* witches spell; magic trick.

apital *adj coll* excellent.

apitally *adv* in an excellent manner, admirably.

aravan *n* non-motorized travel trailer.

arboy *n* large globular glass jar encased in basket-work.

arburettor *n* carburetor.

ardan joint *n* universal joint.

ardigan *n* knitted woolen jacket.

ard-index *n* index file.

ardoon *n* globe artichoke.

ardsharpen *n* card-shark.

areerist *n* one who aims to succeed in business or profession.

aretaker *n* janitor; superintendant.

arking *adj* worrying, harassing.

arman *n* van or truck driver.

ar-park *n* parking lot or garage.

arpet-slippers *n* slippers with uppers made of cloth.

arriage-way *n* road.

arrier bag shopping bag.

arrycot *n* a baby's portable cot.

arry-on *n coll* fuss, silly excitement.

arryings on *n coll* frivolous behavior.

arsey *n sl* toilet.

39

cart, in the *coll* in trouble.

carton *n* cardboard box.

case, put the suppose, assume that.

casebook *n* record kept by doctor, detective.

case-shot *n* shrapnel.

cash & carry discount store.

cashbook *n* salesbook.

cashier *v* dismiss, fire from employment; *mil* dismiss from service dishonorably.

cask *n* barrel.

cast about wander; drift; search.

cat may look at a king even the lowest have some rights; **to make a cat laugh** exceptionally funny.

catapult *n* slingshot.

cat's whiskers, cat's pyjamas *sl* something wonderful.

catch-crop *n* crop sown between two regular, large crops.

catchment *n* drain.

catchpenny *adj* worthless but eye-catching.

catchpole *n* sheriff's deputy, esp arresting for debts.

cat-suit *n* woman's one-piece garment; jumpsuit.

cause-way, causey *n* raised road over marshy area, raised footpath

caught out stuck.

cavenish *n* cake of chewing tobacco sweetened with molasses.

cavil *v* raise trivial objections, quibble.

cellar *n coll* wine collection.

Celt, Kelt (kelt) *n* member of one of peoples speaking Welsh, Breton Erse, Gaelic or Manx.

central heating heating a building by a boiler or furnace as opposed to individually heated rooms.

centrebit *n* wood-boring bit.

centre-reservation median stripe.

centrist *n* one who adopts middle view between extreme positions.

cert *n sl* a certainty; **dead cert** *sl* absolute certainty.

cess *n* assessment tax; **cesspit** *n* cesspool.

chaff *v* tease, banter; **chaffer** *v* bargain, haggle over price; **chaffy** *adv* light, worthless; full of fun.

chaise-longue *n* long couch, sofa.

chamber *n* bedroom; *v* to reside.

chammy-leather *n* chamois or cloth resembling it.

champers (shamperz) *n coll* champagne.

chandler *n* candle maker or seller; **chandlery** *n* place where candles are kept; goods sold by a chandler.

chap *n* man, boy, fellow; **chaps** *n coll* jaws.

chapfallen, copfallen *adj* dejected, crestfallen.

chapman *n* itinerant dealer, peddler.

char *n coll abbr* charwoman; *coll* tea.

character *n* reference.

charabanc *n* carriage.

charade (sharahd) *n* the party game.

charger *n* large flat serving dish; horse of a military officer.

charlie, charley *n coll* utter fool.

charlotte *n* pudding of stewed apple or other fruit mixed with bread-crumbs and baked.

charnel-house *n* vault or place in which bones of the dead are piled.

chartered accountant C.P.A.

charwoman *n* woman who does housework for pay, cleaning lady.

chat up *coll* flatter, amuse by friendly talk.

cheapjack *adj* shoddy, of bad quality.

checkweighman *n* union representative in a coal-mine.

cheek *n* nerve; **cheek by jowl** very close.

cheeky *adj coll* impertinent, impudent.

cheerio *interj coll* goodbye.

cheesed *adj sl* thoroughly bored, depressed, or disgruntled; also **cheesed-off.**

chemist *n* druggist, drug store.

chesil *n* gravel, shingle stones.

chest of drawers bureau, dresser.

chesterfield *n* long sofa with two upholstered ends.

chicory *n* endive.

childminder *n* baby-sitter.

chimney *n sl* heavy smoker.

chimney-breast *n* wall of the chimney that projects into the room and contains the fireplace, damper and flue-pipe.

chimneypot *n* cylindrical pipe of earthenware or metal on top of chimney to prevent its smoking; *coll* top hat.

chine *n* joint of meat consisting of backbone with adjoining flesh.

chink *n sl* money.

chinwag *n sl* conversation, chat.

chipolata *n* spicy sausage, "slim-jim".

chips *n* french fries.

chippings *n* gravel.

chip-shop *n* shop selling fried fish and chips.

chippy *n coll* carpenter.

chirpy *adj coll* cheerful.

chit *n* small child; pert young girl.

chivvy, chivy *v coll* drive along from place to place, forced to keep moving by reminders; nag.

chizz *n v sl* swindle.

chock-a-block *adj, adv* crowded closely together; stuffed.

chocolate *n* chocolate bar or candy.

chokey, choky *n sl* prison.

chop, get the *coll* get fired.

chop-house *n* steakhouse.

chopper, get the *sl* be killed.

chorine *n* chorus girl.

christian name last name.

Christmas-box *n* gift of money given to doormen, servants or tradesmen at Christmas.

chuck it *coll* stop doing that; **chuck up** give up; **give the chuck to** *coll* get rid of, dismiss, break off the affair.

chucker-out *n coll* man employed as a bouncer.

chum *n* close friend; **chummy** *adj coll* friendly; **chumming** ᵥ sharing a flat with a friend.

chunnel *n coll* proposed Channel tunnel between England and France.

chunter *v coll* chatter, mumble; **chuntering along** moseying; driving steady and slow.

Church of England the established church in England, Catholic in faith and order but incorporating many principles of the Protestant Reformation, and independent of the papacy.

churlish *adj* rude, boorish, stingy.

cinder-sifter *n* sieve or grate for coal stove or fireplace.

cine-camera *n* movie camera; **cine-film** *n* movie film.

cinema *n* movie theater.

cinque ports five ports on the English Channel; Hastings, Dover, Sandwich, Romney & Hythe.

circs (surks) *n sl* circumstances.

circus *n* traffic circle.

City, The business or financial heart of London.

city centre downtown.

civvy street civilian life.

cladding *n* wall-covering (exterior).

clan *n* group of families claiming descendency from a common ancestor, esp in Scottish Highlands.

clanger *n* gaffe, mistake,

clapped out *adj sl* worn-out, worthless.

clapper *coll* tongue.

claret *n* red wine of Bordeaux.

claret-cup *n* drink made of iced claret sweetened and flavoured, and mixed with soda water.

clarionet *n* clarinet.

claspknife *n* folding pocketknife.

claspnail *n* cut nail with two points in the head.

claw-hammer *n* ordinary carpentry hammer.

clean-handed *adj* free from blame, reproach; upright.

clean-limbed *adj* well-proportioned in body.

clear-off *vt* get rid of; *coll* get out, beat it.

clearage *n* clearance.

clearing-house *n* central office to clear checks.

clearway *n* road on which there is no stopping.

cleek *n* iron hook; iron-headed golf club.

cleg *n* horse-fly.

clem *v* starve.

clement *adj* gentle, merciful.

clerk (clark) *n* clerk in office or bank.

clever dick *coll* shrewd chap; smart-alec.

climb-down *n* humiliating withdrawal, demotion.

cloakroom *n* checkroom in theater or restaurant.

clobber *n* paste used by shoemakers; *sl* one's belongings.

clog to clog (in three generations) rags to riches to rags.

close *n* enclosure; quadrangle enclosed by buildings; alley leading from street to inner courtyard; **closedown** *n* work stoppage; end of a broadcast day; going out of business; **close-fisted** *adj.* mean, stingy; **close-stool** *n* chamberpot in a chair or stool.

closet *n* small private room; **closet drama** play written to be read and not performed; **water closet** bathroom, toilet.

closing-time *n* hour at which pubs or shops close.

cloth-cap *n* workman; workingman's hat.

clothespeg *n* clothespin.

clotted cream Devonshire specialty of thickened sweet cream.

cloud-cuckoo-land *n* fanciful or ideal place, dreamland.

cloudlet *n* small cloud.

clough (kluf) *n* valley with steep sides, gorge.

clout-nail *n* galvanized roofing nail.

clubland *n* district in the West End of London where the main private clubs are situated.

clubman *n* man about town; member of a club.

clue, not have a be completely at a loss to understand.

clyster *n* an enema.

coach *n* long distance bus; **coach-party** *n* bus trip; **coach-station** *n* bus station.

coals-to-Newcastle do something superfluous, silly.

coal-skuttle *n* enclosed ornamental bucket to carry coals.

cob *n* small lump of coal; roll.

cobbed *v sl* beaten up; snitched on.

cobber *n Aust coll* mate, friend.

cobbler *n* shoemaker.

cock *n sl* nonsense; **go off at half-cock** begin prematurely and ineffectively; **cock-a-hoop** *adj, adv* exultantly, happily; **cock a snook** thumb one's nose; **cock-up** *n sl* mess up, blunder; **cockboat** *n* small boat towed behind a ship or yacht; **cockcrow** *n* early dawn.

cockle *n* edible shellfish; small snail; shallow boat; **warm the cockles of one's heart** cheer up, invigorate.

Cockney *n* person born within the sound of Bow Bells; Londoner; the London East End dialect.

cockshot *n* a toss at an object for amusement.

cockaleeky *n* Scottish soup made with leeks.

codger *n coll* eccentric elderly man.

codswallup *n coll* nonsense, foolishness.

coequal *n* one who is the equal of another; *adj* of the same rank.

coeval *adj* of the same age, period.

coffeebar *n* cafe serving coffee and light refreshment; **coffee-stall** *n* street vendor selling hot coffee, buns.

coign of advantage position giving a good view.

coil *n* noise, turmoil.

cokernut *n coll* coconut.

cold comfort poor consolation, not much help.

coldish *adj* chilly, rather cool.

cole *n* kinds of cabbage; **colewort** *n* cabbage without a heart.

collaborationist *n* traitor.

collar stiffener collar stay.

collaret *n* small collar, piece of lace or fur worn around the neck or throat.

collect *v* call for; pick up.

colleen *n Ir* a girl.

colliery *n* coal-mine.

collop *n* slice of meat; a piece of something.

collywobbles *n sl* stomach-ache; diarrhea.

colour *n* colored badge or ribbon as mark of school, party; **get one's colours** get on the team.

colour-company *n* company carrying the flag of the battalion.

colourist *n* painter, esp water colors; **colourman** *n* one who sells paints.

colporteur *n* bookseller.

combinations *n* union suit.

come off succeed, happen, take place; **come off it!** *coll* stop pretending!; **come round** recover, be reconciled; **come-at-able** *adj* accessible; **come-hither** *adj coll* deliberately alluring; **come to grief** have a spill; a bad time; **come unstuck** to fail; be reduced in rank.

comfit *n* candied sweet.

comforter *n* woolen scarf; bed quilt.

command performance theatrical performance given by royal command and attended by the reigning royalty.

commercial traveler traveling salesman.

commissary *n* delegate, deputy.

commission agent salesman on commission only.

commissionaire *n* uniformed doorman.

commital *n* placing a corpse in a grave or crematory.

commode *n* chamberpot enclosed in a chair; chest of drawers.

common *n* public park or land; **common pleas** small claims court. **common room** living-room shared at boarding school or college; **common-or-garden** ordinary.

commons *n* members of the House of Commons; allowance of food rations. **short commons** insufficient food.

Commonwealth, The The British Commonwealth of Nations, a group of nations and territories united by a common allegiance to the British crown.

companion *n* member of lowest grade of order of knighthood.

compass-plane *n* plane with a curved underside; **compass-saw** *n* tapered hand saw; **compass-window** *n* bow window.

compeer *n* one of equal rank.

compere *n* interlocutor, master of ceremonies.

compo *n* cement-lime mortar.

comprehensive school highschool.

con *v naut* direct course; **conning; conned.**

concierge *n* a clerk in better, older hotels who will book theatre seats, train and plane tickets.

concretize *v* make real or specific.

conductor *n* fare taker on public transportation.

confection *n* sweet, small fancy cake; **confectioner** *n* fancy baker, pastry-cook.

conflate *v* put together readings to form a single text.

Continent, The Europe, the western countries.

Conquest, The The Norman Conquest of England in 1066.

conscience-smitten *adj* remorseful.

consentient *adj* agreeing.

conservancy *n* body of officials appointed to control and protect rivers, forests and open lands.

Conservative party political party founded in 1832 as successor to the Tory party.

conserve *n* candied fruit; jam.

conshy, conshie, conchy *n coll* conscientious objector.

consistory *n* tribunal, council.

consols *n abbr* consolidated annuities in British Government securities.

conspectus *n* survey; analysis.

constable *n* policeman; **constabulary** *n* police force in town or district.

consumer goods goods produced for use in daily life.

container *n* tin can.

continental *adj* pertaining to Europe.

contrariety *n* opposition; inconsistency; setback, hindrance.

contrarily *adv* in a contrary manner; to the contrary; perversely.

cony, coney *n* the rabbit; fur made from rabbit skins.

coo! *coll* exclamation of surprise or disbelief.

cooker *n* stove; **cookery** *n* art and practice of cooking.

cook-out *n* barbecue.

cook the books falsify records.

coomb, combe *n* narrow valley.

coop *n sl* prison.

cop *n* ball of thread wound on a spindle; mound; hillock.

cop it be punished; get into trouble.

copper *n* penny or half-penny.

copper-bottomed *adj naut* sea-worthy; thoroughly safe; genuine.

coppice *n* small forest.

copyline *n* advertising slogan.

copy-typist *n* secretary without shorthand experience.

cor! *interj sl* exclamation of surprise; also **cor blimey!**

corbie *n Scots* crow or raven.

cordwainer *n* shoemaker.

corgi *n* breed of small Welsh dogs.

corn *n* grain; **corn-chandler** *n* retail corn-seller.

cornbrash *n* coarse chalky soil.

corncrake *n* bird with sharp piercing cry.

corn-dolly *n* figure made from plaited cornstalk.

cornflour *n* corn starch.

corn-boy *n coll* loafer.

cornet *n* trumpet; ice-cream cone.

Cornish *adj* of and pertaining to Cornwall; *n* the celtic language of Cornwall; **Cornish cream** thick cream, slightly sourish, served with tea; **Cornish pasty** covered small meat pie; **Cornish wafer** small cookie.

coronach *n Scots* bagpipe dirge or sad tune.

correctness *n* quality of being correct.

corridor *n* hallway.

corrigible *adj* able of being corrected after prison.

corsair *n* pirate; pirate ship.

corvette *n* fast naval escort vessel.

cosh *n coll* small weighted bludgeon or sap; *v* strike with a cosh; render unconscious.

cosher *v* pamper, coddle.

cosset *v* pet, pamper.

cost the earth expensive.

costard *n* large apple variety.

costermonger *n* fruit and vegetable seller usu from a cart.

cot *n* humble cottage; hut; baby's crib; **cot betty** *coll* maid; **cot-case** *n coll* patient too sick to walk.

cottage pie minced meat covered with mashed potatoes and baked.

cottier *n* who lives in a cottage.

cotton *n* thread; **cottoncake** *n* cottonseed used as cattle fodder; **cottonreel** *n* spool; **cottonwool** *n* cotton balls.

couldst *v* can.

council-house, council-flat *n* dwelling built by a local authority and rented to deserving poor; **council-school** *n* school financed locally but public.

counsel *n* advice, guidance; legal adviser, advocate, lawyer; **Queens Council** attorney for the state.

counterblast *n* violent demonstration; aggressive retort.

counterfoil *n* receipt for a bank check.

counter-jumper *n coll* shop assistant.

counterpane *n* bedspread.

county *n* shire or district or state; *adj* pertaining to landed gentry, the rich; *coll* upperclass, socially exclusive.

county college part-time compulsory public school for those 15-18 created under the Education Act of 1944.

county-town *n* administrative center of the county or shire.

courgettes *n* zucchini; squash.

course *n* area of land prepared for races, sport.

coursing *n* hunting by sight; with greyhounds.

court-card *n* picture-cards in a deck; **court-hand** *n* form of handwriting formerly used in documents; **court-plaster** *n* band-aid or tape for cuts and bruises; **court shoe** pump.

cove *n sl* fellow, chap.

coverlid *n* bedspread.

covert-coat *n* short, light overcoat.

cow gum rubber cement, mucilage; **cowhouse** *n* cowshed;

cowpat *n* dung from a cow.

crabwise *adv, adj* moving sideways.

crack on *v coll* give a spurt of speed; **crack up** *v coll* praise enthusiastically.

crackers *adj coll* mad, crazy; *n* fire crackers.

cracking *adj coll* very fast.

crackling *n* crisp rind of port fat.

cracknel *n* light, crisp, puffy biscuit or bun.

crambo *n* game in which one player gives a word to which others seek a rhyme; **dumb crambo** charade in which a rhyming clue is given.

cramfull *adv* full to overflowing.

cramp-iron *n* U-shaped bar to hold up a beam.

cranage *n* the right of using a crane; dues paid for use of a crane.

cranefly *n* daddy-long-legs.

crapulence *n* drunkenness, debauchery.

crash *n* coarse linen used as toweling; **crash-helmet** *n* helmet worn by motorcyclists.

cravat *n* tie; loosely knotted kerchief tied about the throat.

create *v sl* be naughty; act up.

creeper *n sl* ingratiator.

creese, crease, kris *n* Malay dagger.

crepitate *v* crackle, creak, rattle.

crib *n* manger, fodder-rack; small room or house; *sl* house to be burgled.

cribbage *n* card-game for two, three, or four players; **cribbage board** *n* board used for scoring.

cricket *n* outdoor game somewhat similar to baseball, with bats, ball and wickets, with two teams of eleven players each; **cricketer** *n*.

crikey *interj coll* exclamation of astonishment.

crimplene *n* trade name for polyester fabric woven from crimped fiber.

crimpy *adj* frizzy, waved.

crisps *n* potato chips.

croaky *adj* that croaks; harsh.

crock-up *v coll* become a worn-out person; lose health or strength; injure, damage.

crockery *n* domestic utensils of earthenware or china; plates.

crocky *adj coll* broken-down; useless.

croft *n* small enclosed piece of farmable land, generally adjoining a house.

cromlech *n* prehistoric structure consisting of a large flat stone resting on upright ones; circle of standing stones around a mound, like Stonehenge.

crook *n* long stick with hooked end.

cross *adj* angry, irritated, bad-tempered.

crossbench *n* bench in Parliament on which independent members sit.

cross-country *adj, adv* advancing across fields, farms, not by road.

crossing, level *n* intersection of road and railway on the same level, generally controlled by gates. **zebra crossing** *n* crosswalk.

crossly *adv* adversely; irritably, with ill-humor.

crosstalk *n coll* repartee, argument.

crosstie *n* transverse connecting piece; railroad sleeper (log).

crossways *adv* crosswise.

croup *n* rump of horse.

crown *n* representation of the royal line; coin worth five shillings; size of paper, 15 x 20 in.

Crown agents *n* independent office acting as British business agents for foreign administrations; **Crown Colony** *n* colony governed directly from Colonial Office; **Crown Prince** *n* heir to the throne.

crums! *coll* exclamation of surprise.

cry *n* catchphrase, a slogan; **in full cry** pursuing hotly, yelping while chasing, esp with hounds; **hue and cry** pursuit, public anger, uproar; protest; **great cry and little wool** much ado about nothing; **within cry** nearby; **cry off** decline, withdraw from; refuse; **cry up** praise loudly.

crypto- *pref* hidden, secret.

cubbing *n* hunting of foxcubs.

cuddy *n Scots*donkey.

cuff *n* blow with hand or fist; **cuffed** *v* struck.

cul-de-sac *n* dead end.

cully *n sl* fellow, pal.

culver *n* wood-pigeon.

cumber *v* burden, encumber.

cunning *adj* pretty, attractive.

cupboard *n* closet.

cup a tea *coll* easy as pie.

cuppa *n coll* tea.

cup-tie *n* football (soccer) match in competition for a cup, like our World Series or Super Bowl.

curlew *n* wading bird with long slender bill.

curling *n* Scottish game played by sliding flat heavy stones over ice towards a mark.

curmudgeon *n* gloomy, bad-tempered fellow; **curmudgeonly.**

currant *n* raisin.

current account checking account.

currish *adj* like a cur; mean-tempered, quarrelsome.

curse of Scotland the nine of diamonds.

cushy *adj coll* easy, safe, profitable.

cut *v* cause sharp pain or sorrow; *coll* ignore, shun; **cut a dash** make a fine showing; a showy impression; **cut off with a shilling** disinherit.

cute coll tricky.

cutlery *n* knives, usu for the kitchen; flatware used at the table.

cutpurse *n* thief.

cutting *n* clipping (newspaper).

cutty *adj Scots* very short.

cwm (koom) *n* Welsh valley, esp with steep sides; bowl-shaped hollow.

cycle-car *n* three-wheeled automobile; **cycle-clips** *n* pants-clips.

D

dab n small flatfish; adj coll highly skillful, artful; **dabchick** n small freshwater bird.

daft adj foolish, weak-minded; silly; crazy.

daggle v trail in wet grass or mud.

daily n newspaper printed daily.

dalesman n one who lives in a valley, esp in the North of England.

dally v waste time, delay, dawdle; play; **dally with** consider, entertain an idea, scheme.

damfool adj foolish, silly, stupid.

damn-all n nothing.

damned, I'm I'm confused, confounded; you don't say!

dampish adj slightly damp.

danceband n popular music orchestra.

dandle v dance (a child) up and down on the knee.

dandy n naut kind of sloop or cutter.

dandyism n quality of being a dandy, a dude.

darbies n sl handcuffs.

Darby and Joan happily married elderly couple.

dark adj gloomy; secret, mysterious; wicked, evil; **darkly** adv gloomily, dim.

dash expl damn, darn; **dash off** produce hastily; **dashing** adj bold, spirited, showy.

davenport n writing desk.

davy n miner's safety lamp.

day-boarder n child who has lunch at school but lives at home.

dayspring n dawn.

day-return (ticket) n cheapest round-trip fare.

daystar n morning star.

dead-men n empty bottles.

dead-alive; dead-and-alive adj lethargic, depressing; dreary; (of place) where nothing happens.

53

deadlight *n naut* storm shutter over porthole.

deadpoint *n* dead center.

deal in trade in, do business in.

deanery *n* office of the dean.

dear *adj* costly, expensive.

dearth *n* scarcity.

death duties estate taxes.

deathwatch *n* a grub which burrows deeply into timber and makes a ticking noise popularly thought to foretell death.

decent *adj.* respectable, likeable; good enough, passable.

decorator *n* interior house-painter.

deed-poll *n* deed executed by one party only.

deep in absorbed by, heavily into.

deep-laid *adj* well thought-out, planned.

deerstalker *n* close-fitting cap with ear-flaps.

Defender of the Faith a title conferred on Henry VIII by Pope Leo X in 1521, and retained by English sovereigns.

defile *n* narrow valley or gorge.

defoliant *n* spray to kill leaves.

dekko *n, v coll* look; glance; a gander.

dell *n* small wooded valley.

demarara *n* brown or raw sugar.

demister *n* defroster.

demode *adj* out of fashion.

demotic *adj* of the people, common; earthy, vigorous.

demy *n* name of a certain size of paper; scholar of Magdalen College, Oxford.

dene *n* deep wooded valley of a small stream near the sea.

deposit account savings account earning interest.

depressant *n* a sedative; pain-killer; sleeping-pill.

depth psychology psychoanalysis.

Derby (darby) *n* a horse race run annually at Epsom Downs; **Crown Derby** kind of china first made at Derby.

derrick *n* a stationary crane.

derring-do *n* knightly courage; a brave deed.

derv *n* diesel fuel.

desiccated *adj* shredded.

desperado *n* reckless, violent ruffian.

dessert-spoon *n* spoon between a tablespoon and a teaspoon, used for puddings, pies.

destructor *n* trash compactor; incinerator.

detinning *n* recovery of tinplate by chlorine.

deuced *adj, adv coll* confounded(ly), extreme(ly).

devil *n* highly seasoned food, esp broiled; **printer's devil** errand boy in printer's office; **devil a bit** not at all.

devilling cooking with hot spices; do hack work for another.

devil's bible playing cards.

devilish *adv coll* extremely; in a devilish manner.

Devonshire cream thick cream served with tea.

dewpond *n* shallow artificial pond on downland fed by water condensation.

dewy *adj* wet with dew; fresh, soft; refreshing.

dexter *adj* on the right-hand side.

diabolo *n* game played with two sticks connected by a string on which a reel is spun and jerked into the air.

diamonded *adj* crusted with diamonds.

diarist *n* one who writes a diary.

dibber *n* instrument for dibbling; **dibbling** *v* making holes in the ground.

dibs *n* children's game.

dicy, dicey *adj coll* risky, tricky, dangerous; **dicing** *n* dice-play.

dick *n coll* man, fellow; *coll* fool; *n sl* declaration; **take one's dick** take an oath.

dickens *interj sl* the deuce, the devil.

dicky *adj sl* unsteady, shaky; not in good health.

diddle *v coll* cheat, swindle.

digestive *n* stomach pill or preparation; **digestive biscuit** sweet whole-meal cookie.

digger *n* goldminer; *sl* an Australian or New Zealander.

digs, diggings *n coll* lodgings.

55

dike-reeve *n* officer in charge of drains, sluices in the fens.

dim *adj coll* stupid.

dime novel cheap, sensational paperback.

dinghy *n* small pleasure sailing boat.

dingle *n* deep dell, narrow wooded valley; **dingle-dangle** *adj* hanging loosely.

dingo *n* Australian wild dog.

dinkum *adj Aust sl* genuine, honest.

dinky *adj coll* neat, dainty.

dinner suit tuxedo.

diplomatist *n* diplomat.

dipper *coll* pickpocket.

dipso *no adj* dipsomaniac.

dipswitch *n* dimmer to lower or raise headlights.

directly *adv* at once; immediately; shortly, very soon.

directory enquiries telephone information.

directrix *n* female director.

direful *adj* terrible, disastrous.

dirk *n* short dagger usu worn by Highlanders in their sock.

dirtily *adv* in a filthy manner.

disforest *v* clear of trees.

disarmer *n* one who advocates nuclear disarmament.

disbud *v* remove buds from.

discount-broker *n* one who cashes bills of exchange or loans money at a discount on securities.

disculpate *v* free from blame.

dish *n sl* attractive person; **dishy** *adj* lovely.

dishclout *n* dishcloth; *sl* dirty, slovenly woman.

dished *adj* defeated, ruined.

dishmat *n* mat under dishes, tablemat.

dispensary *n* clinic; druggist.

diss *n* fiber used in making rope.

Dissenter *n* Nonconformist, one belonging to a religious body not in conformity with the established church.

district heating system of heating apartments or houses from a central storage heater.

ditchwater, dull as very dull and boring; **clear as ditchwater** obscure.

diversion *n* detour.

dixie *n* iron pot used by soldiers for tea or stew.

DJ *n* dinner jacket.

do *v coll* cheat, swindle, trick; *n* large party or function; **do a bunk** *sl* run away; **do down** get the better of; **do in** *sl* kill; *coll* exhaust; **do in the eye** *sl* swindle; **fair dos** share fairly.

dobby *n coll* fatuous person; fool.

doch-an-doris *n* parting drink, stirrup-cup.

docker *n* longshoreman.

doddle *n* a snap; easy thing.

dodger *n* dishonest person.

dodgy *adj* difficult; tricky; dishonest.

doff *v* take off; set aside; get rid of.

dogdays *n* hottest period of the year.

dogger *n* two-masted Dutch fishing boat.

doggo *adv coll* in hiding, at large.

dog-hole *n sl* mean, disgusting dwelling.

dogs *n* supports for logs or fire-irons in fireplace.

dogsbody *n sl* underling, drudge.

dole *n* food or money given in charity; **on the dole** out of work and collecting unemployment or relief money.

dollop *n coll* large shapeless lump; blob; a serving.

dollar bag soft handbag with drawstrings; **dollar shop** inferior pawn shop; marine hardware store.

dolly-bird *n coll* pretty, young but silly girl.

domestic *n* household servant.

domestic services utilities.

don *n* tutor at college.

done *interj* agreed, settled; **done for** ruined, dying.

donkey's years *sl* a very long time.

doodah *n* state of excitement.

doorstrip *n* small strip of tape or plastic under door.

dormobile *n* camper; VW bus, van.

doss *n sl* bed in a cheap lodging-house; **doss down** arrange a makeshift bed or sleeping arrangement; **doss-house** *n* cheap lodging-house; **dosser** *n* homeless bum.

dot and carry one *coll* walk with a limp.

double-bend *n* S-curve; **double cream** whipping cream; **double-glazing** *n* storm-windows.

dowager *n* prefix assumed by widow of titled man to distinguish her from his heir.

down *n* tract of open, treeless, hilly land.

Downing Street, number 10 residence of the Prime Minister.

downpipe *n* drainpipe.

doxy *n sl* loose woman; prostitute.

draff *n* refuse of malt after brewing; *coll* something worthless.

dragsman *n sl* thief who steals from moving vehicles or trains.

drain *n* soil-pipe.

dram-drinker *n* habitual drinker.

draper *n* cloth or clothing store.

drat *interj coll* bother, confound; **dratted** *adj coll* wretched, infuriating.

draught excluder weather stripping.

draughts *n* checkers.

draughty (drafty) *adj* exposed to, full of, currents of air.

draw the teeth of make harmless.

drawers *n* undershorts.

drawing-pin *n* push-pin.

drawing-room *n* living room, parlor, sitting room.

draw-well *n* shallow dug well.

dreadful *adj coll* bad, unpleasant, tiresome; **penny dreadful** cheap, sensational story or book.

dreary *adj* depressing, boring.

dress circle mezzanine or loge seats.

dresser *n* kitchen piece of furniture with drawers and shelves.

dressing-case *n* traveling case with toilet articles.

dressing-down *n coll* scolding, reprimand; thrashing.

drift-anchor *n* sea anchor; **drift-sail** *n* sail dropped in the sea to check the course of a ship in a storm.

drill *n coll* correct way of doing something.

drill-harrow *n* machine for weeding between rows.

drinking-bout *n* session of serious drinking.

dripfeed *n* intravenous feeding.

drop a brick *coll* make a tactless blunder; a faux pas.

drop down on scold, blame, accuse.

drophead *n* car with a soft roof; a convertible.

dropscene *n* stage backdrop.

drub *v* beat, thrash; abuse violently.

drugget *n* coarse woolen rug.

druid *n* priest of the ancient Celts; officer of Welsh Eisteddfod.

drummer *n* traveling salesman.

dry battery *n* drycell battery.

dryasdust *n* pedantic scholar; *adj* dull.

drynurse *n* baby nurse.

drysalter *n* dealer in salted or preserved foods.

dub up *coll* pay up.

duck *n col!* lovable person; **ducks** *n coll* dear, friendly greeting; white flannel trousers; **ducky** darling, dear.

ducks and drakes game of skipping stones on water.

duff *n* boiled suet pudding; coal dust.

duke *n* holder of the highest hereditary rank of the English peerage; size of notepaper 7 x 10½.

dummy *n theat* actor without speaking part; an extra; rubber pacifier for babies; **tailor's dummy** *sl* showy worthless person.

dumper *n* dumptruck.

dundrearies *n* long side-whiskers; mutton-chops.

dunno *abbr coll* don't know.

durst *v* dare.

dust (a person's) jacket for him *coll* thrash him.

dustbin *n* wastebasket, garbage can; **dustcart** *n* garbage collector's truck; **dustman** *n* garbage collector; *coll* sleep.

dust-up *n coll* commotion, row, fight.
Dutch courage false courage inspired by alcohol; **double dutch** *co*
gibberish, incomprehensible talk.
duvet *n* (doo-vay) down quilt.
dyeworks *n* dye factory.
dynamo *n* generator.

E

each way a bet to win, place or show.

eardrops *n* earrings.

earl *n* English nobleman ranking between a marquis and a viscount.

earldom *n* rank, title, or territorial possessions of an earl.

earnest *n* pledge, guarantee.

earth, go to go into hiding; **unearth** *v* digup; find.

earth-closet *n* out-house; **earthnut** *n* peanut; **earthwire** *n* ground wire.

East Anglia an early English kingdom in SE Britain, now modern Norfolk and Suffolk counties.

eat one's terms study for the Bar.

eating-house *n* cheap restaurant.

echo-sounder *n* depth-sounder.

Edwardian *adj* characteristic of the reign of Edward VII.

eff and blind *sl* swear coarsely; **effing** *adj*.

egg-flip *n* eggnog.

eggwhisk *n* eggbeater.

eiderdown *n* comforter, quilt.

eightsome *n* Scottish reel for eight dancers.

eisteddfod (es-tethvod) *n* yearly assembly of Welsh poets and musicians competing for prizes.

elastoplast *n* band-aid.

elder-wine *n* wine made from elder flowers or berries.

eldritch *adj Scots* weird, uncanny.

elegist *n* writer of elegies.

elevenses *n* morning coffee break.

Elizabethan *adj* relating to Elizabeth I or to her times; characterized by ornament of German or Flemish origin.

Emerald Isle Ireland.

enchase *v* set or frame in; engrave, emboss.

end *n* the very best, the last word; **latter end** old age; death; **no end** *coll* extremely; **on end** without stopping; **wrong end of the stick** complete misunderstanding.

endlong *adv* lengthwise; on end; vertically.

end-use *n* final use for which a product has been designed.

endways *adv* on end, upright; pointing forward.

engaged *v* occupied; (phone) busy.

engaging *adj* attractive, pleasant.

engine-driver *n* locomotive engineer.

English *adj* of, pertaining to, or characteristic of England or its inhabitants, institutions, or language; The people of England as distinguished from those of Ireland, Scotland, and Wales.

entrain *v* put into or onto a train; board a train.

ephedrin *n* drug used for low blood-pressure and hayfever.

ergo *adv* therefore.

erk *n* new recruit.

Erse *n* Irish Gaelic; Scottish Gaelic.

escritoire *n Fr* writing desk.

escutcheon *n* shield bearing a coat of arms; **blot on one's escutcheon** stain on one's reputation.

espalier (Espalyer) *n* trellis.

Esperanto *n* an international language.

esquire *n* address of an untitled gentleman.

Establishment, The The Church of England; upper classes.

estate agent real estate broker or salesman; **estate car** station-wagon.

Estates, The Three Archbishops and Bishops, Peers, and Commons.

Eton crop woman's very short hair style.

euchre *n* a card game.

even up balance; **even up on** retaliate against; get even; **even-handed** *adj* impartial, fair.

evidence, queen's state's evidence.

excellency *n* title of honour given to ambassadors, viceroys, governors of colonies and their wives.

exchange *n* place where city merchants, bankers and brokers meet to transact business, mostly trading in stocks.

exchequer *n* treasury; **Chancellor of the Exchequer** finance minister of the British government, equal to the Secretary of the Treasury.

exhibitioner *n* student with a maintenance grant.

exon *n* officer of th Yeomen of the Guard.

express *n* special delivery; **expressly** *adv* plainly; directly; especially.

ex-serviceman *n* veteran.

extempore (extempery) *adj* unprepared.

ex-works *adv* from the factory.

eye *n* metal loop to tie clothing; bud, shoot (of plant); **all my eye** *coll* nonsense; **do in the eye** *sl* cheat, spoil; **keep one's eyes skinned** be very careful.

eyebath *n* eyecup; **eyebright** *n* kind of small white flower; **eyeglass** *n* monocle; **eyeshot** *n* range of vision.

eyewash *n* humbug; pretense; flattery.

F

Fabian Society organization founded in England in 1884 favoring the gradual spread of socialism by peaceful means.

fabulist *n* writer or teller of fables.

face *n* boldness, impudence; **have the face to** be bold or impudent enough to; **fly in the face of** flout; **pull a face** grimace.

faceache *n* neuralgia; *sl* gloomy or unpleasant-looking person.

face flannel wash cloth.

facer *n coll* strong blow in the face; difficulty, problem; card facing the wrong way in a pack.

factor *n Scots* estate manager.

faddist *n* one who has fads.

faddy *adj* having fads.

faff *v coll* dither, waver; **faff about** be inefficient.

fag *n* cigarette; **fagged, fagging** *v* tired, exhausted; **fag-ends** *n* worthless bits.

faggot *n* liver, chopped, seasoned and baked.

fain *adj* ready, willing, glad to.

faintish *adj* somewhat faint.

fair *n* periodic gathering for display and sale of goods, often accompanied by amusements, competitions, bazaars; trade exhibition.

fair-faced *adj* lovely; hypocritically charming.

Fair Isle *adj* type of knitting design named after a Shetland island.

fairy-lamp; fairy-light *n* small colored lamp used as decoration; **fairy-ring** *n* circle of noticeably darker grass.

falconry *n* hunting with and training of falcons.

faldstool *n* folding-stool.

fall *v* lose power in business or office; **fall about** *sl* laugh wildly; **fall away** desert; **fall in with** happen to meet; agree, comply with; **fall out** quarrel; **fall over backwards** make extreme efforts; **try a fall with** pit oneself against.

fallal *n* finery.

falsework *n* temporary framework; scaffolding.

faltboat *n* collapsible kayak; folbot.

famous *coll* excellent, first-rate; **famously** *adv coll* very well, excellently.

fancy *n* enthusiasm; **fancy dress** costume for masquerade; **fancy man** *sl* man living on a prostitute's earnings; pimp; **fancy woman mistress, prostitute; fancy that!** imagine that!; **fancy work** embroidery.

fanfaronade *n* brag, bluster.

fanny *n sl* female vulva; **sweet fanny adams** nothing; zero.

fantast *n* dreamer or visionary.

far and away very much.

farce *v* stuff, season, spice; force-meat.

farrier *n* one who shoes horses; blacksmith.

farthing *n* former bronze coin equal to 1/4 of a British penny.

fash *v* annoy, vex.

fast and loose behave irresponsibly.

fat *n* best part of anything; **the fat is in the fire** trouble is on the way; **a fat lot** *coll* nothing at all, don't believe it.

Father Christmas Santa Claus.

feather industry one sheltered or subsidized by the government.

feather-bed *v* pamper, shield from hardship; limit work or output in order to avoid dismissing redundant workers.

featly *adv* nimbly, gracefully.

feckless *adj* careless, reckless.

fell *n* hill or mountain side.

feeze *v* screw in, twist in; *coll* disturb, alarm; *n coll* agitation, fuss.

feller *n* one who cuts down or that which fells, trees.

felloe, felly *n* wheel rim.

fellow-feeling *n* mutual understanding, sympathy.

femineity *n* feminity, womanliness.

fen *n* low-lying marshy land.

fender *n* metal guard to span open fireplace or hearth.

Fenian *n adj* of Irish nationalism; working for overthrow of British rule.

fenny *adj* marshy, boggy.

feretory *n* shrine for relics; tomb; bier.

fernery *n* place for growing of ferns; masses of ferns.

ferny *adj* of, like, or containing ferns.

ferriage *n* conveyance by, fare for, a ferry.

ferro-concrete *n* ferro-cement; reinforced concrete.

fetch *v* go to, get and bring back; cause to come; **fetch** *n coll* trick, dodge; apparition or double of a living person; spectre.

fetch and carry run errands.

fetching *adj coll* attractive.

few, some; not a few; **a good few** a fairly large number.

fey *adj* fated to die, about to die; *coll* whimsical.

fibreboard *n* wall-board made of pressed wood fibers.

fiddle *v coll* fidget, play aimlessly with; move restlessly; waste time; *sl* sell or buy illegally; wangle.

fiddler *n sl* cheat, rogue; sixpence; smallcrab.

fieldclub *n* society for open-air nature study.

field fare *n* hat similar to deerstalker but without flaps.

field glass binoculars.

field officer *n* officer above rank of captain and below general.

fight shy of avoid.

figure of fun person who looks ridiculous.

filibuster *n* pirate, adventurer.

fillet steak sirloin steak.

film *n* movie; **film star** movie star.

finnan haddie smoked haddock.

finnoc *n Scots* white trout.

finny *adj* having fins; fin-like; of, teeming with fish.

fire, hang *coll* be slow, delay; **set the Thames on fire** achieve a great success.

fire-brigade *n* fire dept.

firedog *n* andiron; **fireguard** *n* fireplace screen; **fire-irons** *n* andirons.

fireship *n* burning ship sent among enemy vessels to set fire to them.

first *n* highest university degree; **first-floor** *n* storey above ground floor; our second floor; **first-foot** *n* first person to enter a house in the New Year; **first night** *n* opening night of play, film.

firstrate *adj* of best quality.

firth *n* estuary; fjord.

fish, cry stinking disparage oneself; **pretty kettle of fish** *coll* muddle, trouble.

fish and chips fried fish and french fries made usu in chip shops only to take-out, sometimes spiced with vinegar.

fish-hawk *n* the osprey; **fish-kettle** *n* long oval saucepan; **fishmonger** *n* one who sells fish; fish market; **fishpaste** *n* small sandwich spread made of fish; **fishslice** *n coll* spatula.

fit-out *n coll* equipment, outfit.

fitted *adj* built-in; **fitted carpet** wall-to-wall.

fit-up *n theat* makeshift scenery and props; touring troupe using this.

fiver *n coll* five-pound note.

fivescore *n* a hundred.

fizzer *n coll* something first-rate.

fizzy *adj* that fizzes.

flag *v* droop, hang limply; grow weak, diminish.

flag-day *n* day on which money is collected for charity by selling small paper flags or emblems to contributors.

flagging *n* pavement of flagstones.

flag-lieutenant *n* admiral's aide; **flag-officer** *n* admiral.

flagwagging *n coll* semaphore signalling; aggressively patriotic.

flaming *coll* bloody; damned.

flan *n* round shallow open tart, usu fruit-filled.

flank speed the full speed of a ship.

flap *n* disturbance; noise; **flapdoodle** *n* nonsense.

flapjack *n* flat powder compact; pancake.

flat *n* apartment; **block of flats** apartment building; **that's flat** that is final, plain, or certain; **go flat out** *coll* move or act fast, strive hard.

flat-iron *n* clothes iron.

flatlet *n* two or three-room apartment; studio apartment.

flatly *adv* plainly, bluntly.

flattish *adj* somewhat flat.

flautist (*flaw*tist) *n* flutist.

flaw *n* sudden squall.

flay *v* beat; strip off the hide from; critize severely.

flea in one's ear sharp rebuke.

fleapit *n coll* fleabag, shabby, dirty room, building.

Fleet Street in London, to mean the British press; newspapers.

flesh-hook *n* meathook.

fleshly *adj* pertaining to the body; carnal, sensual.

fleshpot *n* pot for cooking meat; luxury greatly wished for.

flex *n* electric cord.

flick-knife *n* switch-blade.

flicks *n coll* movies.

flight, put to rout, utterly defeat.

fling in one's teeth reproach, taunt with.

flintglass *n* brilliant glass containing lead silicate.

flipper *n sl* hand, limb.

flirty *adj* inclined to flirt.

flite *v Scots* quarrel, abuse, scold.

flittermouse *n* a bat.

flockbed *n* bed stuffed with wool or cotton waste.

flockpaper *n* flocked wallpaper.

flog *v coll* sell; **flog a dead horse** waste one's efforts.

flogging *n* punishment by beating.

floorcloth *n* cloth for washing floors; mop.

floorer *n coll* question or remark that astounds, confounds.

florin *n* British silver coin worth two shillings or 10 new pence; gold coin of Edward III worth six shillings & eightpence.

fluky *adj* of or by unexpected good luck.

flummery *n* almond-flavored blancmange or cake; *coll* humbug, nonsense.

flummox *v coll* confound, disconcert, puzzle.

flunkey *n* man-servant in livery (uniform); toady, servile flatterer.

fly at attack vigorously; **fly in the face of** defy; **fly in a rage** grow suddenly angry.

flyboat *n* swift canal barge; **fly-book** *n* case holding angler's flies; **fly-fishing** *n* fly casting; **flying-bridge** *n* pontoon bridge; **flying-fox** *n* large fruit-eating bat; **flyman** *n* stagehand who works the flies; **flyover** *n* overpass; **flypaper** *n* sticky paper to catch insects.

fob *n* small pocket in vest or pants to carry a watch; *v* cheat; **fob off** delude or trick into accepting worthless articles.

fogbank *n* mass of fog resting on the sea.

foggy *adj* vague, confused.

fog-lamp *n* foglight.

foie gras (fwah-grah) pate.

folklorist *n* student of folklore.

folkweave *n* loosely woven fabric.

follow-on *n* second innings of cricket immediately after the first.

fondant *n* soft sweet which melts in the mouth.

foolscap *n* size of writing paper; typing paper.

football *n* soccer; soccer-ball.

footboard *n* sloping board against chassis on which driver rests his feet; board at foot of the bed.

footer *n sl* game of soccer.

footmuff *n* warmly lined bag for warming feet; **footpad** *n* thief who robs on foot; mugger; **footrule** *n* 12 inch ruler; **footslog** *v sl* tramp, march.

foppery *n* affectation, foolish vanity.

forby, forbe *prep, adv Scots* besides; near by; past.

forcemeat *n* meat chopped fine and seasoned, used for stuffing.

force-pump *n* water pump.

foreign minister British member of cabinet similar to Secretary of State.

Foreign Office the British State Department.

foreshore *n* part of shoreline between high and low water mark.

foretime *n* old times, the past.

forgo; forwent; forgone *v* refrain or abstain from, renounce.

forked stick muddled, unstable person.

form *n* established custom; **good (bad) form** socially (un) acceptable.

forswear *v* renounce solemnly; swear falsely; perjure oneself.

fortnight *n* two weeks.

fosse *n* ditch; moat.

fossway *n* old roman road.

fossick *v coll* hunt around, rummage; *Aust sl* search for gold over-looked by others.

foul *adj* very dirty, filthy; disgusting; stormy; tangled; very bad; obscene; **fall foul of** collide with.

foulness *n* quality of being foul.

Founder's shares stock given to original subscribers.

four-ale *n* ale formerly sold at fourpence a quart; **four bar** a pub.

fourgon *n* baggage truck.

four-in-hand *n* carriage with four horses driven by one man; kind of loose-flowing necktie.

fourpence *n* sum of four pennies.

fowling-piece *n* light shotgun, around 20 gauge, for shooting birds.

foyer (foy-ay) *n* lobby, entrance hall, esp theater.

frangipane *n* almond-flavoured pastry; perfume made from red jasmine.

franglais (frong*lay*) *n* modern French incorporating English words.

frank *n* postage cancellation mark on envelope or stamp.

franklin *n* small landowner.

frank-pledge *n* ancient system of establishing a community.

frappe *(frapay)* *n* iced, cool; dessert made of frozen fruit juice.

freakish *adj* capricious; eccentric; extraordinary; grotesque.

Free Church Scottish Presbyterian Church; Nonconformist Church.

free house pub not dependent upon one brewery.

free-handed *adj* generous.

freehold *adj* land free of encumbrances, leases.

freeliver *n* one rejecting moral restraints, esp re sex.

french bean stringbean; **french leave** AWOL; **french letter** pro-phyactic; condom.

frenchify *v* make french, ornate, frilly, in appearance.

frenchy *n coll* french person.

fresh *adj coll* slightly drunk; cheeky.

fresher *n coll* first-year undergraduate.

fret *v* erode; corrode; ruffle; complain; **fret** *n* a state of anxiety.

fridge, frige *n coll abbr* refrigerator.

Friendly Society mutual insurance company.

fringe *n* tassles; bangs (hair).

frippery *n* tawdry finery; showy knick-knacks; affected elegance.

frisky *adj* playful, lively.

frizz *v* curl or crisp (the hair); **frizz** *n* crisp, tight curl.

fritz *n coll* German soldier.

frock *n* long outer coat; woman's dress; monk's robe.

frog *n* ornamental loop and button on clothes; leather attachment to belt supporting a sword or dagger; *coll* frenchman.

Front Bench one of two benches in the House of Commons occupied by Ministers or by leading members of the Opposition.

frou-frou (*froo*froo) *n* rustling of silk; elaborate decoration.

frowsty *adj* hot airless, stuffy; musty, ill-smelling.

fruit-machine *n* slot-machine.

fruiterer *n* fruit seller or stall; fruit market.

frummel *v coll* fry.

frump *n* dowdy, badly dressed woman.

fry-up *n coll* mixture of foods fried together.

fubsy *adj* fat and stumpy.

fuddle *v* confuse the mind esp by drink; become stupidly drunk.

fug *n coll* stuffy atmosphere; dust, fluff.

fuggy *adj* stuffy, airless.

full age adulthood; **full marks** top grades; excellent job; **full round** sandwich, esp in pubs; **full stop** absolute stop; punctuation mean-ing end of sentence, piece; **full cry, in** hot pursuit of.

fully-fashioned *adj* seamed and shaped (usu stockings).

fumous *adj* smoky.

fundament *n* the buttocks; anus.

funnel *n* metal chimney; smokestack.

funnily *adv* in a jocular or amusing way; oddly; **funnily enough** strange to say, but.

furnisher *n* furniture store; one who sells furniture.

furze *v* spiny evergreen shrub, similar to gorse.

G

gab *n* talkativeness; *sl* mouth; **gift of the gab** facility, talent at speaking.

gaby *(gay*by) *n* fool, simpleton.

gad! *interj* my! well!; *n* wanderer; **on the gad** moving from place to place.

Gael *n* Scottish or Irish Celt; **Gaelic** *n, adj* (language) of the Gaels or Irish.

gaff *n sl* nonsense; **blow the gaff** *sl* divulge a secret.

gaffe *n* blunder.

gaffer *n* boss; captain; chief.

gagster *n* joke-teller.

gainsay *v* contradict; deny; oppose.

gaggle *adj* flock; bunch (of women).

gallery *n* long, narrow passage; *theat* balcony seats; audience occupying those seats.

galluses *n coll* suspenders.

galumph *v* leap about clumsily; swing about joyfully.

game *adj* crippled, limply; **gammy**.

gamester *n* gambler.

gammer *n* old woman.

gammon *n* smoked or cured ham.

gamp *n coll* large umbrella, named for Mrs. Gamp in Dickens' Martin Chuzzlewit.

ganger *n* foreman.

gangway *n* aisle.

gannet *n* goose.

gaol *(jail) n* prison; **gaoler** *n* prison warder, guard.

garage *(gar*-ij) gas station; garage.

garn *inter sl* exclamation of disbelief or wonder.

garret *n* attic.

Garter, The highest order of knighthood; badge of this order.

gasbag *n coll* talky person; windbag.

gas-cooker *n* cooking stove.

gas-fitter *n* person who installs or repairs gas appliances, pipes.

gasper *n sl* cheap cigarette.

gateau *(gat*O) *n* fancy cake.

gawp *v sl* stare stupidly.

gay *adj* lively, cheerful, merry; bright in hue; showy.

gazump *n* snafu; *v* raise price after agreeing to lower one.

gear *n* tools, apparatus, equipment; *sl* clothes.

gear-box *n* transmission; **gear-lever** gearshift.

gee-up *interj* exclamation urging horse on: gittup!

gel *n* (gel†) girl.

gemmy (jemmy) *adj* set with gems; sparkling.

gen *n sl* the truth; correct info: **gen up** *sl* learn quickly.

gentrification *n* upgrading a run-down area or town.

gentry *n* upper-class people not belonging to nobility.

gents *n coll* men's public lavatory.

George *n* name of six kings of England, the last, George VI, father of Queen Elizabeth II; *sl* any coin bearing the image of St. George; **by George** exclamation of wonder.

Georgian *adj* of the period of any of the Georges.

German silver alloy of cooper, nickel and zinc.

german *n* kind of tunafish.

get along with you *coll* beat it, go away; nonsense.

get-at-able *adj* accessible.

get cracking *coll* move swiftly; get to work now; **get sorted out** arrange things; get settled; **get stuffed** *exclam* drop dead.

getting on growing old.

geyser *n coll* gas water heater.

ghastly *adj* terrifying, hideous; ghostlike.

gherkin *n* small sweet pickle.

ghyll, gill *n* ravine, gully; brook.

Gib *n abbr* gibraltar.

gib *n* tomcat; castrated cat.

giggle *n* something for fun alone.

gigolo *n* hired male dance-partner; lover living off his mistress.

gillie *n Scots* outdoor servant or attendant on a hunt.

gilt-edge *adj* of the highest quality.

gimlet *n* small tool for hole-boring.

gimp *n* twisted and stiffened cord of silk for trimming.

gin-fizz *n* drink made from gin, soda and lemon.

ginger up *coll* brighten, make livelier.

ginger-pop *n coll* ginger beer.

Girl Guide like the Girl Scouts.

giro *(jiro) n* checking account system.

git *n sl* bastard, despicable person.

give over cease, transfer; **give rise to** cause; **give tongue** talk, cry; **give to** addicted to; **give way** yield.

gladsome *adj* cheerful.

glass *n* mirror; **glasscloth** *n* fiberglass cloth; cloth for cleaning glass; **glasshouse** *n* greenhouse, hothouse; **glass-wool** *n* fiberglass insulation.

Glaswegian *n, adj* of Glasgow.

Glauber's salt *n* a purgative; sodium sulphate.

glaze *v* fit with glass; **glazier** *n* glass-cutter.

gleeman *n* minstrel.

glengarry *n* boat-shaped Scots Highland cap.

glitch *n sl* sudden stoppage of machinery; a monkey wrench in.

glorification *n coll* a festivity.

glory-hole *n* cupboard or small closet where garbage accumulates.

glover *n* one who makes or sells gloves.

glow-lamp *n* battery powered lamp, or lantern.

gloze over explain away.

glozing *n* flattery.

gluey *adj* like glue, sticky.

go *n* try, attempt; **goer** *n* good or quick worker; **go down** *sl* leave school, university; be believed; **go over** *sl* make an impression; **have a go** try, make attempt.

gods *n coll* cheapest, highest seats.

gonk *n* comic-looking doll.

goodish *adj* quite good, fair.

goodman *n Scots* householder; husband.

goods *n* merchandise; **goods train** freight train.

good show! well done!

goodwife *n Scots* housewife.

goody *n* heroic or faultless character in movie or book.

goose *sl* silly girl, foolish person; **goosego** *n coll* gooseberry.

gormless *adj* dim-witted, stupid.

gorse *n* prickly yellow-flowered shrub, usu in the West Country; **gorsy** *adj* thickly grown with gorse.

go-slow *adj n* slowdown at the factory.

gossoon *n Ir* servant boy; lad.

governor *coll abbr* (governor) father; old man; the boss; sir.

gowan *n Scots* daisy.

gowk *n* cuckoo, *coll* simpleton.

Grace, Your mode of address to duke, duchess, or archbishop.

grammar school secondary school.

grammercy *interj* thank you.

gramophone *n* record player.

grampus *n* person who breathes or wheezes loudly.

gran *n coll abbr* grandmother.

grant *n* students are entitled to it according to need.

grapy *adj* of or like grapes.

grass *n coll* snitch; **grass-snake** *n* harmless British snake.

graver *n* engraver.

greaseproof paper wax paper.

Great Britain since 1707 the name applied to the British Isles.

great unwashed, the the proletariat, great majority.

greats *coll* final Honours School of Humanities at Oxford.

grebe *n* tailless diving bird.

greedy-guts *n sl* glutton.

green belt area around a town where building is forbidden; **green finger** green thumb; **greengrocer** *n* retail vegetable and fruit market.

griddle *n* broiler.

grig *n* grasshopper.

grill *n* to broil; **grill-room** *n* steakhouse or room in restaurant for broiling.

gripe *v* feel crampy.

griskin *n* lean bacon.

groats *n* hulled grain.

grockles *n* summer visitors.

groom *n* officer of royal household.

grotty *adj sl* bad, unpleasant.

grouse *v* complain, gripe.

grub-street *n coll* hack writer, writing.

guard *n* railroad conductor.

Guards *n* five regiments of the Queen's household.

gubbins *n coll* any complex machine or apparatus; simpleton, fool.

guidepost *n* signpost.

Guild hall *n* a hall of the Corporation of the City of London.

gum *n* liquid glue.

gup *n coll* gossip; chatter.

guy *n* effigy of Guy Fawkes.

Guy Fawkes Day November 5, celebrating the capture of Guy Fawkes, by setting a bonfire in the middle of the village green.

gyp *n sl* give (someone) **gyp**; give pain.

H

hab-dabs *n coll* nervousness; jitters.

haberdasher *n* retail store dealing in ribbons, thread.

hack *n* horse let out for hire; overworked horse.

hackney *n* rented horse.

haft *n* handle to knife, sword, dagger.

haggis *n* Scottish dish of sheep's inner organs mixed with oatmeal, seasoned and boiled in the sheep's stomach-bag.

ha-ha *n* unseen ditch; sunken fence.

hair dresser barbershop.

hair-grip *n* bobbie pin; **hair-lacquer** *n* hairspray; **hairslide** *n* barrette; **hair-tidy** *n* small box for combed-out-hairs.

half *n coll* half pint of beer; **too clever by half** far too smart; **not half!** *sl* very much so; **not half bad** *sl* very good.

half-pace *n* stair landing; **half-round** *n* half sandwich.

half two, four 2:30, 4:30.

hall, the village squire's residence.

halt *n* stop.

hammer, come under the be auctioned; **go at it hammer and tongs** set to work vigorously; quarrel violently.

hammer-cloth *n* cloth or sheepskin covering driver's seat.

handbag *n* woman's pocketbook; **handbill** *n* printed notice, advertisement; **handbrace** *n* drilling brace.

hang about linger, loiter.

hang-it-all; let go hang not care a damn.

Hansard *n* official printed report of Parliamentary proceedings.

Hanse *n* medieval guild; **The Hanse** commercial association of various free towns.

hansom *n* horse driven cab formerly used in London.

ha'penny *n* half penny.

haply *adv* perhaps.

ha'p'orth (hayperth) *n abbr* a halfpennyworth.

happy as Larry overjoyed.

hard, the ashore; on land; **hard cheese** tough luck; **hard by** close; **hard at it** hard at work.

hard-bound *adj* hardcover (books).

hark back retrace one's steps.

harridan *n* disreputable old hag.

hasp *n* metal clasp; handle; door-handle.

hatted *adj* wearing a hat.

hatter *n* hat-store; hat maker; **mad as a hatter** eccentric; crazy.

hat-trick *n* in cricket, act of taking three wickets with successive balls; similar fear in any sport.

haulier *n* trucker; **road-haulier** long-distance trucker.

have it attack; make a try.

having one on kidding, tricking; **not having any** none for me.

hawk *v* sell things door-to-door or with a pushcart; **hawk about** spread news, tell secrets; **hawking your mutton** *sl* prostitution.

hawker *n* peddler, esp one with pushcart.

head, give one his allow one complete freedom; put one in charge.

headlamp *n* headlight.

headmaster *n* principal of a school.

heart, pluck up take courage.

heartsease *n* wild pansy; peace of mind.

heartwhole *adj* not in love.

hedgerow *n* hedge.

heel, down at shabby; **come to heel** (of dog) to heel; **lay by the heels** capture; **show a clean pair of heels** to escape.

heist *v sl* steal cars.

heller *n* trouble-maker; **hellish** *adv coll* very unpleasantly; sticky.

henna *n, v* rinse or dye for hair, to dye one's hair.

herb (hurb) *n* plant used medicinally or to flavor foods.

hern *n* heron.

herring, red interesting but irrelevant fact used to divert attention from the main topic.

hessian *n* burlap.

79

hide, have a thick thick-skinned.

hew *v* cut down, as with an ax; chop; hack at; carve with an ax.

hidebound *adj* rigidly conventional; narrow-minded.

hiding *n coll* a thrashing, beating.

higgledy-piggledy *adv, adj* in disorder; all a jumble.

high *adj* (of meat) slightly spoiled; **high colour** ruddy complexion; **ride the high horse** behave arrogantly.

High Court British supreme court.

high tea early supper with tea, served around 6; mostly in the north counties.

Highland Fling Scottish dance.

highminded *adj* having fine ideals or principles.

hind *n* peasant, farm-worker; skilled farmer; bailiff.

hip-bath *n* portable bath-tub.

hire *v* rent, esp cars; **hire-purchase** to buy on installment.

hit off describe briefly, accurately; *sl* go away, beat it; sketch rapidly; **hit it up** *sl* behave badly.

hive off *v* allocate production to a subsidiary.

hob *n* hearth ledge to keep things hot.

Hobson's Choice either what is offered, or nothing.

hock *n* German white wine.

hodden *n Scots* coarse undyed woollen cloth; **hodden grey** mixture of black and white wool.

hogg, hogget *n* yearling sheep.

hogmanay *n Scots* New Year's Eve; festivities held at that time.

hoick *v* raise or rise abruptly; jerk up; lift.

hokey-pokey *n* cheap ice-cream.

hold-by be guided by; maintain, stick to.

holdall *n* large bag or case.

holding *n* piece of land or investment held.

hole, in a in trouble.

hole-and-corner *adj* furtive, underhand, sly.

holiday *n* vacation; **Bank Holiday** national holiday; **holiday-maker** *n* vacationer; tourist.

holland *n* kind of coarse linen; **Hollands** *n* kind of Dutch gin.

hols *n coll* school vacations.

Home Counties counties nearest London; **Home Guard** reserve force of part-time volunteers; **Home Office** Government department dealing with domestic affairs.

homely *adj* pleasant; kind, good natured.

honor bright *coll* truly, without deceit.

honors list Queen's list of those receiving titles or honors.

hood *n* collapsible, convertible top for car.

hoo-ha *n coll* noise; quarrel.

hooks, go off the go mad, crazy; behave wildly.

hooper *n* maker and repairer of barrels, casks.

hoot *n* something silly; **hooter** *n* car-horn.

hoover *v coll* clean with vacuum cleaner.

hop *n* dance; **hop it** *sl* go away, beat it.

hop the twig *sl* die; evade one's creditors.

hop-o-my-thumb *n* pygmy, dwarf.

horn *n* telephone; **get on the horn** *v* call.

Horny, Old the devil.

horse, flog a dead work for a lost cause.

horsebox *n* horse-van; **horsecloth** *n* horse blanket; **horsecoper** *n* horse-dealer of doubtful honesty; **horse furniture** saddlery.

Horse Guards *n* household cavalry, headquarters in Whitehall, London.

horse-marines *n* imaginary force of naval cavalry; **tell it to the horse-marines** *coll* expression of incredulity.

horsy *adj* high interest in horses, riding.

hosier *n* store selling hosiery; **hosiery** *n* men's underwear, socks, collars, ties.

hot on keen on, expert in.

hotchpotch *n* thick mixed stew; confused mixture, jumble.

House, the *abbr* House of Commons, Parliament.

house-agent *n* real estate salesperson.

houseboy *n* African or Asian domestic servant in a white man's home.

housecoat *n* woman's elegant dressing-gown.

housefather *n* warden of a reform school; older boy responsible for helping a young newcomer at school.

houses, safe as quite secure.

housing estate subdivision.

House of Lords nonelective upper House of Parliament.

housemaid's knee inflammation of kneecap.

housey-housey *n* game of chance resembling lotto or bingo.

howl down prevent one from being heard by shouts of mockery.

hoy *n* large single deck boat; small boat for transportation to and from ship.

hue and cry angry pursuit; outcry, uproar.

hugger-mugger *n* insincerity, hypocrisy; kind of peppermint.

humbug *n* nonsense; a kind of candy.

hundredweight *n* 112 lbs.

hunkers *n Scots* buttocks; **on one's hunkers** squatting.

hunks *n coll* surly old man; miser.

hunting-box *n* hunting cabin.

hurley *n Ir* hurling.

hurling *n* Irish game resembling hockey; Cornish ball-game.

hurst *n* hillock; sandbank; copse.

hush-hush *adj* very secret.

hypermarket *n* very large supermarket, usu out of town.

I

ice *n* ice cream; **iced lolly** popsicle.
identification parade *mil* line-up.
identikit *n* composite picture of unidentified person.
idler *n* lazy fellow; loafer.
ill-bred *adj* bad mannered; **ill-gotten** *adj* obtained dishonestly; **ill-humoured** *adj* bad-tempered; **ill-judged** *adj* unwise; **ill-starred** *adj* unlucky, disastrous.
immediate *adj* with nothing coming between; next, very near.
imperial *adj* pertaining to the British Empire; fixed as a standard throughout the Empire; *n* a small beard on chin.
imshi *interj sl* go away!
inappetence *n* lack of desire.
inbeing *n* essence; basic nature.
inbuilt *adj* built-in; innate; inbred.
inchmeal *adj* very gradually.
inch-tape *n* tape-measure.
incommode *v* cause inconvenience or trouble to; embarrass; disturb; **incommodity** *n* inconvenience.
incondite *adj* badly constructed; confused; unfinished.
inconstant *adj* variable, changeable; fickle; unsteady.
incontinent *adj* unrestrained, lacking self-control, esp over sexual passion.
Indian *adj* pertaining to India; **Red Indian** American Indian.
india-rubber *n* eraser.
indirection *n* indirect course; dishonest means.
indolent *adj* idle, lazy; inactive.
indomitable *adj* that cannot be mastered; unyielding.
indubitable *adj* that cannot be doubted; quite certain.
inelastic *adj* rigid; unadaptable.
inexact *adj* not precise, accurate.

inexpiable *adj* that cannot be atoned for.

inflexible *adj* unbending, unyielding.

infrequent *adj* not often; rare, unusual.

ingle-nook *n* chimney corner.

ingratitude *n* lack of gratitude, manners.

inhospitable *adj* not kind; giving no shelter; bleak.

iniquitous *adj* very wicked; unjust.

initially *adv* at the start.

inky *adj* like ink; black.

inlander *n* one dwelling inland.

inland Revenue Internal Revenue.

inly *adv* inwardly; intimately; sincerely.

Inns of Court four legal societies through one of which a person may be admitted to the bar; buildings of these societies.

inoffensive *adj* giving no offence; harmless.

inquire, enquire *v* ask questions.

insect screens screens.

insincerity *n* quality of being false, insincere.

inspector *n* police officer just below the rank of superintendant.

intelligencer *n* secret agent.

intemperate *adj* not moderate; violent, excessive; lacking self-restraint.

interiorly *adj* in or towards the interior; privately, inwardly.

interloper *n* intruder; meddler.

interpol *n* international police force, throughout Europe.

interurban *adj* between cities and towns.

interval *n theat* intermission between acts.

intrepid *adj* fearless.

intuitionalism *n* philosophical doctrine that truth is only known through intuition.

inverted commas quotation marks.

invincible ignorance ignorance which one cannot remedy by one's own efforts.

Irish *n adj* of Ireland.

Irish English the standard language of Ireland.

Irishism *n* custom, manner, practice characteristic of the Irish.

Irish stew stew usu made of mutton, lamb or beef with potatoes onions, etc.; **Irish tweed** sturdy fabric of light warp and dark filling used in men's suiting; **Irish whiskey** whiskey made in Ireland of barley.

iron-grey *adj, n* of the color of iron freshly broken.

ironist *n* one who uses irony.

ironmonger *n* hardware store; store selling tools, metals.

ironware *n* goods made of iron; hardware.

isabella *n, adj* greyish yellow.

issue, at in dispute, under discussion.

J

jab *n coll* shot (injection).

jabber *v* speak quickly and confusedly, gabble.

jack it in stop trying; **every man-jack** everyone; **jack-leg** jerry-built; **I'm all right Jack!** the devil with you!; **jack tar** sailor; **Union Jack** flag of Great Britain.

jackanapes *n* mischievous boy; conceited person, fop.

jacket potato baked potato.

jack-in-office *n coll* pompous or bullying petty official.

jack-in-the-green *n* man inside leaf-covered framework at May Day festivities.

jackstraw *n* straw effigy; nonentity.

jacob *n sl* ladder.

Jacobean *adj* of or pertaining to James I or his period.

Jaffa *n* large orange grown in Israel.

Jag *n coll abbr* Jaguar car.

jam jelly; **jam on it** pleasing surplus; **jampot** jar.

jammy *adj coll* lucky; **dead jammy.**

jankers *n sl* military prison.

jannock *adj* genuine; straightforward, excellent.

jaw *v, n sl* talk at length; a long conversation.

jawbreaker *n* difficult word.

jelly *n* Jello.

jemmy *n* burglar's crowbar.

jerkin *n* man's close-fitting leather jacket; short vest.

jerry *n sl* chamber-pot; **jerry-builder** *n* speculator who builds cheap houses.

jersey *n* a sweater.

jiggered *adj coll* amazed; **I'm jiggered!** I'm surprised!

jiggery-pokery *n coll* trickery, underhand dealing.

jimmy riddle *n sl* a piddle (urinate).

jingo *n* one aggressively patriotic; warmonger; **by jingo!** *coll* exclamation of surprise.

job, just the exactly what one wants.

jobbery *n* corrupt practice in public positions.

jogtrot *n* slow steady trot; jog.

John Barleycorn alcoholic beverages; **John Bull** the English people; typical Englishman; **John Collins** drink of gin, lemon and soda; **John Thomas** *coll* penis.

johnny *n coll* young fellow, chap; dandy.

joiner *n* furniture-maker.

joint *n* section of meat as cut ready for cooking; a roast.

jointer *n* bricklayer's pointer.

joking, you're you're kidding!

jolly good you're all set; fine; **jolly well** very; **jolly** *adj* gay, in high spirits; *n naut coll* a Royal Marine; **jollyboat** *n naut* ship's boat; **jolly hockeysticks** good show!

jollification *coll* party, merry gathering.

jove, by! *coll* exclamation of surprise.

judy *n sl* woman, girl; ridiculous person esp woman; **make a judy of oneself** *coll* play the fool.

jug *n* pitcher.

juggins *n coll* simpleton, idiot.

julienne *n* clear meat soup with finely chopped vegetables; kind of pear.

jumble sale garage sale, rummage; **jumble shop** second-hand store.

jump the queue obtain service, goods out of one's turn; push ahead.

jumper *n* woman's sweater.

junior school grade school.

K

kaput *adj coll* broken, finished; dead, out of order, not working.

keek *v, n Scots* peep.

keen *adj* sharp, having good cutting edge; acute; very sensitive; **keen on** eager, ambitious for; very fond of.

keep it dark keep it quiet, secret; **keep your wool on** don't be angry; **keep your hair on** wait a minute; **keep your pecker up** be cheerful.

ken *v Scots* know; recognize.

Kentish fire rounds of applause or dissent.

kerb n curb; **kerb-crawling** *n, adj* driving slowly along to pester women pedestrians.

kerfuffle *n sl* fuss; panic.

kibosh *n sl* rubbish, nonsense; **put the kibosh on** *sl* put an end to, prevent.

kick about lie neglected; **kick against the pricks** do oneself harm in rebelling; **kickshaw** *n* toy, trifle; elaborately cooked dish; **kick-up** *n coll* row, commotion; a party; **kick up a shindy** make noise; **kick one's heels** wait impatiently.

kilderkin *n* barrel containing 16 gallons, or two firkins.

kilo *n abbr* kilogram.

kilt *n* Highland Scotsman's pleated usu tartan knee-length skirt.

kingbolt *n* chief bolt; kingpin connecting front axle to body.

King's English educated or correct speech.

kiosk *n* pay telephone booth; newsstand; cigar stand.

kip *n sl* bed; lodgings; sleep.

kipper *n* smoked herring.

kirby grip bobbie pin.

kiss the dust bite the dust, die.

kiss of life mouth-to-mouth resuscitation.

kit *n* outfit, equipment; set of tools: small wooden tub.

kitchener *n* cooking stove.

kitchen-garden *n* vegetable garden.

kitchen-sink *adj theat* plays showing sordid, ordinary aspects of life.

kittle *adj Scots* requiring careful handling.

knacker (nacker) *n* person who buys old unfit horses, houses or ships; to break them up for scrap; **knackered** *adj sl* exhausted; worn out; useless; **knackers** *n sl* testicles.

knag (nag) *n* knot in wood; knob, peg.

kneepan *n* kneecap.

knees up *coll* party, shindig.

knickerbockers *n* loose breeches; knickers.

knickers *n* woman's undergarment.

knight *n* commoner holding a personal non-hereditary dignity conferred by the sovereign and carrying with it the title Sir; **knight bachelor** lowest rank among British knights.

knightly *adj* of or like a knight; chivalrous; valiant.

knock against meet by chance; **knock back** *sl* swallow; startle; **knock up** call upon; telephone.

know-all *n* busybody.

knuckleduster *n* brass knuckles.

L

label *n* tag.

Labour Day celebrated in Britain on 1 May; **Labour Party** political party of moderate Socialist views in Britain.

lace-ups *n coll* shoes or boots fastened by laces.

lackey *n* liveried (uniformed) manservant.

lacklustre *adj* dull, dim.

lad *n* boy; young man; *coll* man of dashing and often wild character; **laddie** *n Scots* lad.

ladder *n* stocking-run.

la-di-da *adj coll* giving oneself superior airs; high-class; affected.

Lady *n* title of wives of baronets, knights, and peers below the rank of Duke; **ladyship** *n* condition or status of lady.

ladybird *n* ladybug.

lady-in-waiting *n* attendant to a lady of royal rank.

lady's fingers okra.

lag *n coll* convict or ex-con, esp one who has been to jail often.

lager *n* type of light beer, similar to American beer.

lagging *n* covering material for pipes, boilers etc; insulation.

laid on ordered, arranged.

laird *n Scots* landowner.

Lake Poets Wordsworth, Coleridge & Southey, so called from their residence in the Lake District.

lallans *n, adj* speech of the Lowlands of Scotland.

lame *adj* crippled; inadequate, unconvincing.

lampoon *n* violently abusive satire.

land-agent *n* person employed to manage an estate; real estate broker.

landloper *n Scots* tramp, vagrant.

landrover *n* sturdy car like a jeep, often with steel cover.

lantern slides slides.

larder *n* pantry.

large-hearted *adj* sympathetic, generous, charitable; tolerant.

largish *adj* somewhat large.

lark *n* joke; prank; **larky** *adj* playful, mischievous.

larrikin *n Aust sl* young hooligan.

lash-up *n coll* hasty improvisations; jury-rigged.

lass *n* girl, sweetheart.

lastly *adv* finally; in the end.

latch-key *n* key for the main door of a house; house-key; **latch-key child** schoolchild whose home is normally empty when he returns.

lather *n coll* thrash, beat severely.

latitudinarian *n, adj* person of liberal views in religious matters.

latterly *adv* recently.

launder *v* wash and iron linen (tablecloths, napkins, etc.) and clothing.

lavatory *n* room fitted with sink and toilet.

law, go to start a lawsuit.

Law Lords peers qualified by judicial experience to deal with legal questions in the House of Lords.

lawn-tennis *n* tennis.

lay *v* set (table); **lay aboard** *naut* come alongside.

lay by set aside, discard; store up; places where cars may stop along highways; **lay by the heels** imprison; catch.

lay in gather stores (supplies) of; *n* nap.

lay oneself out put oneself out.

layfigure *n* jointed model of the human figure used by artists.

lazy-tongs *n* extendable tongs to lift things at a distance.

leading article editorial.

leal *adj Scots* loyal, true.

learnt *v* p/part of learn.

leathern *adj* of or like leather; tough.

leave, French AWOL.

leave-taking *n* act of saying goodbye, esp ceremoniously.

left-luggage office baggage room.

leggo *exclam coll* let go!

leggy *adj* long legs.

leg show *theat* entertainment specializing in nude or nearly-nude female participants.

legman *n* traveling sales man or reporter.

let *v* lease, rent.

letterbox *n* mailbox; **letter-carrier** *n* mailman.

level crossing railroad crossing.

Libertarian *n* one who holds idea of the freedom of the will.

libertine *n* person who habitually leads an immoral life.

licensed *adj* authorized to sell liquors.

lichgate *n* roofed gateway to a churchyard.

lick and a promise quick superficial washing or other job.

lie-down *n coll* short rest.

life peer peer whose title is not inherited.

Life Guards two cavalry regiments acting as bodyguards to British Sovereign.

lift *n* elevator; **liftboy, liftman** *n* elevator boy, man.

lighter *n* flat-bottomed boat similar to landing barge.

light-minded *adj* frivolous.

lily-white *adj* very white; much loved.

limey *n* British sailor; Englishman.

limited liability company (Ltd.) a corporation.

linchpin *n* axlepin.

line of country bailiwick, territory.

line, ship of the battleship; **shoot a line** *sl* boast; **get a line on** find out about.

linen-draper *n* fabric store.

liner train freight train.

links *n* golf course.

lino *n abbr* linoleum.

linsey-woolsey *n* fabric of coarse wool and cotton.

literalism *n* insistence on following text word for word.

litterbin *n* trash basket in streets; **litterlout** *n coll* litterbug.

little-ease *n* cage or cell in which one can neither sit nor lie down.

little-go *n coll* preliminary exams at Cambridge U.

liver sausage liverwurst, braunsweiger.

liverish *adj* irritable.

livery *n* distinctive uniform worn by servants of one employer.

loaf *sl* head.

loath *adj* unwilling; **nothing loath** quite willing.

lobby *n* hall; corridor; waiting-room where Members of the House of Commons and their constituents can meet.

loblolly *n naut* gruel; **loblolly boy** surgeon's assistant.

lobscouse *n naut* meat and vegetable stew.

local *n* one's nearest pub.

loch *n Scots* lake.

lock-up *n* time for locking up; *sl* prison.

lodging *n* accommodations; rooms rented in private house.

lollop *v coll* move by clumsy bounds; bob up and down.

lolly *n coll* lollypop; *sl* money, esp won.

longcase clock grandfathers clock.

long wave FM.

long-headed *adj* shrewd; **long-sighted** *adj* prudent, foresighted.

longways *adv* lengthwise.

loo *n coll* toilet, bathroom.

loofah *n* bath scrubber.

look alive make haste; **look sharp** be alert or energetic.

looker-on *n* onlooker, spectator.

look-in *n coll* chance to take part; chance of success; hasty glance.

looking-glass *n* mirror.

loon *n Scots, coll* boor, lout; fool; puffin.

loony-bin *sl* lunatic asylum.

loose chippings loose gravel (on road).

lop *v* chop off; shorten.

lord *n* peer, nobleman; member of the House of Lords, upper chamber of British Parliament; **my lord** form of address to peers.

lord; good lord; my lord exclamations of surprise, dismay, wonder.

Lord Chancellor chief judge of England.

lord luv a duck *sl* exclamation of surprise.

Lord Mayor mayor of London or certain other cities.

lordling *n* young or pretty lord.

lords and ladies wild arum, a weed.

lordship *n* power or jurisdiction of a lord; **your lordship, his lordship** formal mode of address.

lorry *n* large truck, usu open; **lorry-hop** *v sl* hitch-hiking via truck; **lorryload** *n* as much as a truck can hold.

lost-leader *n* goods sold at a loss to attract customers; **lost, get coll** beat it, go away; **lost on** having no influence on; wasted on; **lost property** lost and found.

lot, the total mount; all there is; **fat lot** not a chance.

loudhailer *n* bull-horn.

lounge *n* comfortable sitting room, living room; **lounge bar** the slightly more decorated, and expensive, side of a pub; **lounge lizard** idle hanger-on; **lounger** *n* idler; **lounge suit** business suit.

lout *n* coarse, ill-mannered person; **loutish** *adj*.

lovey *n sl* darling.

low, bring humiliate, degrade; ruin.

low church evangelical Church of England; **low comedy** farce; burlesque. **lowborn** *n, adj* born of humble parentage.

lower house House of Commons.

lowermost *adj* lowest.

lowlands *n* southeastern region of Scotland; **lowlander.**

loyalist *n* one who remains loyal to the government in times of revolt; **Ulster Loyalist** one who supports the union of Ulster with England.

lubber *n* clumsy, stupid fellow; *naut* untrained seaman.

lucky bag, lucky dip grab-bag.

Luddite *n* one of a band of English workmen who tried in 1811-16 to prevent industrialization by wrecking factories and machinery.

ludo *n* game played on a checker board with counters and dice.

lug *n coll* ear; potholder, handle.

lugger *n* small vessel with lug-sails.

lumber *n* large objects; disused furniture; rubbish, trash; rough planks; *v* clutter with trash; overload; worry, burden.

lumber-room *n* attic or cellar room where unused furnishings are stored.

lumme, lummy *interj sl* exclamation of surprise; well, I'll be!

lump *n coll* dull, stupid person.

lump it *coll* put up with something unpleasant.

lumpish *adj* shapeless; clumsy; stupid.

lustily *adv* vigorously, heartily.

lustrous *adj* shining, radiant.

luv *n sl* term of endearment; address by many tradesman and women, esp in market stalls.

lyceum *n* building housing a literary society.

lying-in *n* confinement, childbirth.

M

macadam *n* hard-surfaced road, named after Scot J. L. McAdam.

mackintosh *n* raincoat; **mac.**

mad *adj* insane, mentally disordered; frantic; crazy; wild; foolish.

madding *v* make angry, become angry.

madcap *n* wild or rash.

maffick *v* celebrate uproariously.

mag *n coll abbr* magazine; magneto; magpie; talkativeness.

Magna Charta (magna *kar*ta) the great 'charter' of English liberties forced from King John by the English barons, and sealed at Runnymede, June 15, 1215.

maiden speech first speech in Parliament of a new member.

mail *n Scots* tax; rent; tribute.

main, in the on the whole; **main** *n* cockfight; (dicing) stake; throw; **mainbrace** *n naut* brace of a main yard; **splice the mainbrace** serve out double ration of grog; **mainmast** *n naut* principal mast; **mainsail; mainsheet.**

mains *n* electricity.

mainspring *n* chief motive for, source of action.

maisonnette *n* part of a house used as a self-contained dwelling.

maize *n* corn.

majordomo *n* manager of a royal or large household.

make at move quickly towards; **make away with** kill, destroy; steal; **make for** go towards; attack; tend towards; **make off with** steal.

makeweight *n* something added to make up required weight; thing or person of small value used to fill a gap.

maladroit *adj* awkward, clumsy.

mall *n* broad alley or avenue; **The Mall** (mal) a road into St. James's Park.

malmsey *n* a sweet white Madeira wine.

Malthusian *adj* advocating control of the growth of population.

mam *n coll abbr* mother; madam.

man, old *coll* father; old friend; **to a man** without exception; **man and boy** since boyhood; **man of the world** man with much experience.

manacle *n, v* handcuff.

manager *n theat* producer.

Mancunian *n* of, from Manchester.

mandarin English excessively formal style.

mangel-wurzel *n* large coarse beef.

mangy *adj* having the mange; mean; shabby; sordid.

manifestly *ad* obviously, clearly.

manikin *n* Little man, dwarf; lay figure; tailor's dummy.

man-jack, every everybody.

mannequin *n* woman model of clothing.

manner: all manner of all kinds of; **by any manner of means** at all cost; **in a manner** to some extent.

mannerly *adj* with good manners.

manor *n* estate consisting of house and ancient rights over land possessed by the owner; *sl* area supervised by one unit of a police force; **to the manor born** naturally well-fitted for upper class environment; spoiled.

manor-house *n* home of owner of a manor.

man-trap *n* trap of two steel claws to catch trespassers or poachers.

Manx *adj* of or in the Isle of Man; **Manx cat** tailless breed of cat.

many-sided *adj* having many talents, interests.

map, off the inaccessible; *coll* unimportant; **put on the map** make famous.

Marchioness *n* wife or widow of a marquis.

mare, shanks' one's own legs; walking.

marge *n coll abbr* margarine.

marguerite *n* black-eyed Susan; ox-eyed daisy.

mark you mind you; matter of fact; **beside the mark** irrelevant; **up to the mark** of required standard; excellent.

market-day day in which a market-town holds its weekly outdoor market; **market-garden** *n* garden in which produce is grown to sell.

market-town *n* town in which a weekly public market is held.

maroon *n* West Indian Negro.

marquee *n* large tent.

martini *n* dry white vermouth only; **dry mart.**

marquis, marquess *n* rank of nobility just below that of duke.

marrow *n* squash.

marry up marry above one's station.

marsh-gas *n* methane.

mash tea *coll* make tea.

mashie *n* golf club used as pitching or sand wedge.

masque *n* dramatic entertainment consisting of tableaux and dancing; may have dialogue and songs.

massy *adj* weighty; solid; bulky.

master *n* teacher; ship captain; **master-mariner** *n* captain of merchant ship.

masterstroke *n* plan carried into effect with signal success.

mat, on the *coll* in trouble.

matchboard *n* tongue-in-groove boards.

materially *adv* in a material way; importantly.

matey *adj coll* friendly, sociable.

maths *n coll* mathematics.

matily *adv coll* in a friendly fashion.

maulstick *n* padded knobbed stick used as a painter's hand-rest.

maunder *v* speak vaguely and disconnectedly.

mavourneen *n Ir* darling; dear.

mawkish *adj* over-sentimental; feebly emotional; sickly, insipid.

Maying *n* celebration of May Day festivities.

mayn't *coll abbr* may not.

May Week week in early June when festivities and boat-races are held at Cambridge U.

mazy *adj* like a maze; puzzling.

mead *n* alcoholic drink made of fermented honey.

meadowsweet *n* plant with white fragrant flowers.

mean *adj* shabby, dingy; inferior; stingy.

mean mischief intend something malicious.

means-test *n* inquiry into financial resources of a person seeking unemployment benefits.

measure, made to clothes made individually to measure; **measure one's length** fall flat; **measure swords** fight.

meat-safe *n* small cupboard for storing meat.

medico *n sl* doctor; med student.

medium wave AM broadcast band.

meetly *adv* fittingly.

Member of Parliament elected representative in House of Commons.

mental defective any individual unable to profit from schooling.

mercer *n* dealer in fabrics and cloth.

mere *n* pool, lake.

merkin *n* artificial vagina.

Merovingian *adj* of the first dynasty of frankish kings established by Clovis about 500 AD.

mess about spend time idly; potter about; work untidily; fiddle with.

messmate *n* one who eats at the same table.

metalled surface paved road.

meths *n coll abbr* methylated spirits; denatured alcohol.

mettle *n* courage; vigor, ardor; **on one's mettle** eager to succeed.

mews *n* converted stables now dwellings.

Mick, Micky, Mickey *n sl* an Irishman; **take the mickey out of** mock, tease; insult.

mickle *adj Scots* great, large.

midden *n* dunghill; pile of trash.

middlebrow *n* taste intermediate between high and lowbrow.

middle class *adj, n* of or in the middle, neither aristocratic nor working class; **lower middle class** including shopkeepers, self-employed artisans; **upper middle class** including landowners, members of the professions, etc.

Middle English English language of period c1150-1475.

middlemost *adj* nearest the middle.

middling *adj* mediocre; moderate.

midge *n* small gnat or flying insect.

midmost *adj, addv* in the very center.

mike *v sl* be idle.

milady *n* my lady.

milkbar *n* ice-cream parlor.

milkshake *n* drink of whisked and flavored milk.

milksop *n* effeminate coward.

mileometer *n* odometer.

mill about go around and around; move about haphazardly.

mince *v* to chop (meat) etc. into very small bits; *n* hamburger; **mincer** *n* meatgrinder; **mincepie** *n* pie made with chopped meat.

mind *v* pay attention to; be wary; take care; **mind you** matter of fact.

mingy *adj coll* miserly; worthless.

mini *n* type of small car; **mini-cab** *n* private cab.

mint sauce sauce of chopped mint, sugar, vinegar, and water.

miry *adj* mucky, muddy, swampy.

misbegotten *adj* illegitimate; badly organized; dishonest.

mischief *n* naughtiness; annoying but not wicked behavior.

miserly *adj* like a miser, avaricious.

misgiving *n* fear; suspicion, anxiety.

miss, give it a *coll* omit, avoid, leave alone.

mitten, get the *coll* be jilted.

mizzle *n, v* drizzle; *sl* go away.

mmm! *interj* what? you don't say! ho–hum; eh? look at that! oh yes

mo *n coll abbr* moment.

mod *adj sl* up-to-date; elegant; dandified youth.

mod cons *abbr* modern conveniences; plumbing, elect., etc.

Modern English the language since 1475.

modish *adj* fashionable, smart.

mog, moggie *n sl* cat.

mole *n* breakwater, jetty; artificial harbour.

mollycoddle *v* pamper.

monarchy, constitutional monarchy, such as Britain's, where the sovereign's power is limited by law.

money box piggy bank.

Money grubber *n* avaricious man; ambitious to get rich.

onger *n* trader, dealer.

onkey *n sl* rogue, mimic; 500 pounds or dollars; **get one's monkey up** *sl* get angry; **monkey tricks** mischief; **monkey-engine** *n* piledriver; **monkey-jacket** *n* sailor's pea-jacket; **monkey-nut** *n* peanut in shell; **monkey-puzzle** *n* tree with spiny leaves and branches.

onstrous *adj* shocking; absurd; hideous; malformed.

ooch *v coll* loiter, hang about; saunter idly.

oonlighter *n* Irish Land League terrorist.

oor *n* wild-stretch of open country usu elevated and covered with heather, coarse grass, bracken.

orning coat tails; **morning room** parlor used in the morning.

orphia *n* morphine.

orris *n* type of English folk dance.

other wit common sense, inborn or native intelligence.

otor *n coll* a car.

otorbike *n* motorcycle.

otorcar *n* automobile; **motoring** *n* act or habit of driving a car; **motorist** driver.

otor-spirit *n* gasoline.

otorway *n* superhighway.

ountebank *n* buffon; imposter; charlatan; quack doctor.

ousse *n* frozen cream and gelatin dessert.

oving staircase escalator.

ow *n, v* grimace; a face.

uch of a muchness very similar.

uck in with *coll* share lodgings, rations; **make a muck of** *coll* bungle; make dirty; **muck about** *coll* behave idly or mischievously.

uckle *n Scots* large quantity.

uckleheap *n* manure pile.

ucksweat *n* profuse perspiration.

uff *n* one clumsy at sports; fool; milksop; blunderer.

ufti *n* civilian clothes; out of uniform.

ug *n sl* fool; easy mark; **mug punter** horse-better.

uggins *n sl* fool.

mugwump *n sl* one who sits on the fence esp in politics.
mule millinery harness, saddlery.
mules *n* heelless slippers.
mum *n coll abbr* mother.
mumbo-jumbo *n* something idiotically venerated.
mummery *n* mime-show; meaningless ceremony.
mush *n* radio jamming.
music-hall *n* comic vaudeville or variety show; theater for this.
muslin *n* cheesecloth.
mustard, keen as enthusiastic.
muzzle *v* restrain; silence.
muzzy *adj* dazed; vague; tipsy.
my word! exclamation of surprise.

N

naafi *n* PX, canteen.

nab *n sl* catch; arrest; steal.

nail-varnish *n* nail-polish.

nancy; nancy-boy *n sl* effeminate youth, homosexual.

nap *n* racing tip.

napkin *n* linen napkin (not paper).

napoo *adj sl* good for nothing; done for, finished.

nappy, baby's nappy *n* diaper.

nappy *adj* strong, heady (of ale).

nark *n* police informer; **nark it** stop it; keep quiet.

narky *adj sl* bad-tempered, sarcastic.

narrowly *adv* closely; only just.

nasty *adj* dangerous, threatening; **turn nasty** become spiteful; **nasty bit of work** very unpleasant, dangerous task or person.

national service draft into armed services.

National Trust British charitable body for preserving buildings or land of outstanding beauty or historic importance.

natter *v, n coll* chatter; grumble; gossip.

nave *n* hub of wheel.

navvy *n* digger on road construction, railroads, sewers.

nearside *n* left-side (curb).

neat *n* ox, cow or bull; *adj* drink straight.

necessitarian *n* one who believes that all human actions are determined by laws of causation, and not by free will.

neck or nothing recklessly.

neckcloth *n* tie; **neckerchief** *n* cravat worn around the neck.

nelly *n sl* effeminate youth; **nelly, not on your** certainly not.

Nessie *n coll* an alleged prehistoric monster inhabiting Loch Ness in Scotland.

nether limbs legs.

never-never *n coll* on installment.

new penny British coin introduced in 1971, worth one hundredth of a pound.

newmarket *n* a card game.

newsagent *n* shop selling newspapers, etc. Our proverbial candy, cigar store.

next *adv* the nearest, most immediately following; *prep* nearest to.

nibs, his *sl* smart gentleman; the boss.

niblick *n* (golf), a sand-wedge.

nick *n sl* prison; **Old Nick** the devil; **in good nick** *coll* in good health or condition; **nick in** slip quickly into another's place.

nicker *n sl* guinea; pound sterling.

niff *v sl* small nasty.

nifty *adj coll* smelly, swift, agile; fine; clever.

niggle *v* fuss over petty details.

nignog *n pej sl* Negro or other dark-skinned person.

niminy-piminy *adj* too dainty or affected; prudish.

nip *v sl* steal; catch in the act; *n* pinch; bite; sudden frost; **nip along** go quickly.

nissen hut quonset hut.

nit *n sl* nitwit, fool.

nix *n sl* nothing; no.

nob *n sl* head; fine gentleman.

nobble *v* cheat, fix a race; kidnap.

nobbut *adv dial* nothing but.

nobby *adj sl* smart, stylish.

nod through accept quickly and without discussion; **on the nod** on credit.

noddle *n coll* the head.

no-go *n* restricted area.

noggin *n* mug, cup; small amount of liquor.

nonce; for the nonce temporarily; for once.

nonstarter *n* person who has no chance of competing successfully

non-stick *dj* teflon-coating.

104

non-U *adj coll* belonging to or used by the upper class; bad form in language, manners.

noodle *n* fool.

Norfolk jacket loose jacket with pleats and belt.

Norman *n* member of the French-Scandinavian race who conquered England in 1066; **The Norman Conquest.**

Norman architecture 11th & 12th century style of English architecture.

nose to tail one behind the other; **nose on** *sl* inform against; **nose out** detect by smelling; discover.

nosegay *n* bunch of small flowers.

nosey parker inquisitive person; busybody.

note *n* paper money; **notecase** *n* wallet; **notepaper** *n* writing paper.

not to worry don't worry.

nought *n* zero; **noughts and crosses** tic-tac-toe.

nowt *n dial, coll* nothing.

number-plate *n* license plate.

nut, do one's *sl* behave wildly through anger.

nutcase *n sl* madman; fool.

nutter *n sl* madman.

O

oafish *adj* foolish; stupid; loutish.

oar; put one's oars in interfere; **rest on one's oars** relax.

oast house building for drying hops of beer.

obit *n abbr* obituary.

oblige *v* bind, compel; necessitate; *coll* do as a favor to; work for.

occasion, on when necessary; **rise to the occasion** be equal in an emergency.

odd *adj* surplus, to spare; **odd job** casual work, single job; **oddment** *n* remnant; something left over; small trifle; **oddness** *n* strangeness.

odds-on *adj* better than even (chance).

off *adj* remote; unlikely; unlucky; inactive; decaying; tainted.

off, I'm so long; I'm going

offchance *n* slight possibility.

offence *n* breach of law or custom.

offhandedly *adv* casually.

offish *adj coll* aloof, distant, cool.

off-license *n* license to sell liquor to take out.

off load *v* load up.

off-putting *adj coll* disconcerting, causing dislike.

offscourings *n* rubbish; worthless parts.

off-the-peg *adj* ready-made clothes, not made-to-measure.

ogreish *adj* foul, moody.

oil the palm of bribe.

oilbox *n* greasebox attached to wheelhub.

Old Bailey *coll* the high court in London.

old bean, boy, chum, cock, egg, fellow, friend, gel, girl, hat, job, lad, man, pip, pot, rip, salt, shoe, son, sport, stick, top friendly form of address.

old boy network help from one's own class in business.

old hat out of date; obsolete.

old stager old hand.

one-off *n* done or made just, once.

onfall *n* an attack, onset.

ongoing *adj* still existing or progressing; not completed.

open eyed *adj* vigilant; wary; **open-handed** *adj* generous; honest.

open into lead into, give access to.

opera-cloak *n* woman's long cape; **opera-hat** *n* man's collapsible top hat.

operating theater operating room; **operator** *n* surgeon.

oracle, work the obtain one's end by intrigue.

order about bully, dominate.

ostler, hostler *n* inn-servant in charge of the horses, carriages.

otherness *n* state of being separate and distinct; alien, different.

ouch *n* jeweled pin or buckle.

out, flat with great speed or strength of effort.

out of it *coll* excluded, isolated, finished.

outface *v* stare boldly at; defy successfully.

outfitter *n* haberdasher; men's clothing store.

outhouse *n* detached outbuilding.

outmost *adj* outermost.

outsize *adj* extra-large.

out-of-door *adj* outdoors.

oven-cloth *n* potholder.

overdraft *n* act of overdrawing an account.

overleaf *n* next page.

overly *adv Scots* too much.

overtake *v* pass.

overmuch *adj, adv* too much.

overshoes *n* rubbers, boots, galoshes.

over the road across the street.

owlish *adj* stupidly solemn; with a fixed stare.

Oxbridge *adj, n* of Oxford and Cambridge Universities.

Oxonian *n adj* of Oxford; the best English.

P

pack (cards) *n* deck.

packet *n* parcel, package; *sl* large sum of money; heavy blow; heavy punishment; trouble.

pack it in give up, cease.

packing, send dismiss abruptly; be fired.

packing-case *n* large wooden box.

packman *n* peddler.

paddle *v* walk barefoot in shallow water.

paddy *n coll* burst of anger; Irishman; **paddywhack** *n coll* burst of anger; smack.

pah *interj* exclamation of disgust.

paid, put *coll* put an end to; prevent.

paint pot paint can.

panama *n* light hat of undyed straw.

panda car police car.

pandy *n coll* stroke of a cane; a caning on the hand; **pandybat** *n* thick, stiff leather strap for beating schoolboys' hands.

pantechnicon *n* moving van.

panto *n coll* pantomime; comedy play based on a fairy tale and performed around Christmas season.

pants *n* men's undershorts.

parade *n* raised promenade along a seashore; boardwalk.

paraffin *n* alcohol; **liquid paraffin** mineral oil laxative.

paraffin oil kerosene.

parboil *v* to boil.

parcel *n* small package.

parget *v* cover with plaster.

parky *adj sl* chilly.

Parliament *n* the legislature of Great Britain, consisting of the House of Commons and the House of Lords.

parlour *n* living-room.

parson *n* minister of the Church of England; **parson's nose** *coll* rump of a cooked fowl, chicken.

part, take in good accept with good humor.

partridge *n* small British gamebird.

pash *v dial* crush; hurl; *n sl* sentimental attachment; hero worship.

pass, bring to cause; **pass out** graduate.

passage *n* hall-way.

pass-key *n* master-key.

pastrycook *n* baker.

pasty *n* meat pie in pastry and baked without a dish, usu found in pubs and coffeebars.

patball *n coll* tennis badly played.

patch *n* territory, bailiwick; **patch, bad** *coll* period of difficulty or unhappiness; **not a patch on** *coll* very inferior to.

patently *adv* obviously, clearly.

patty *n* small meat pie.

pavement *n* sidewalk.

pawky *adj* shrewd, sly.

paypacket *n* pay envelope; **paysheet** *n* payroll.

pearlies *n* large mother-of-pearl buttons.

pease *n* peas; **pease pudding** peas split, boiled & mashed.

pebbledash *n* wall surfacing by spraying gravel on wet plaster.

pecker *n* spirits; **keep your pecker up.**

peckish *adj* hungry.

peer *n* person of equal rank or merit; one entitled to sit in the House of Lords; **life peer** one whose peerage does not pass to his heir.

pelican *n* traffic light controlled by pedestrians.

pemmy *adj* pudgy.

pence *n* pl of penny.

pen-friend *n* pen-pal.

penn-orth *n coll* pennyworth.

penny-a-liner *n* inferior journalist.

penny dropped, the finally!

peppercorn *adj* small, insignificant.

perisher *n* fellow; **perished** *adj* worn out.

perry *n* drink of fermented pear-juice.

personal call person-to-person.

perspex *n* plate-glass used in windshields; plexiglas.

pertly *adv* in a cute way.

petrol *n* gasoline.

pi *adj sl* pious.

pick holes in find fault with.

pickaback *adv* piggy-back.

pickers and stealers petty thieves.

picking *n* petty theft; scraps of food; trifles left over.

pickle *n* pickled relish.

picklock *n* thief who picks locks.

pick-me-up *n* tonic, stimulant.

Pickwickian *adj* simple, endearing, kind.

picture house, picture palace cinema, movie.

pidgin *n* business, job.

pie *n* magpie; species of woodpecker.

piece of cake *sl* easy.

piece up patch up.

pier-glass *n* full-length mirror.

piffle *n* nonsense, rubbish.

piffling *adj* ridiculous, nonsensical; petty.

piggery *n* pigsty; dirty or untidy room.

pignut *n* peanut.

pig's ear mess up; *sl* beer.

pi-jaw *n sl* speech on religion or morals.

pile-up *n coll* multiple-car crash.

pillarbox *n* mailbox.

pillion-passenger *n* one riding behind driver on motorcycle.

pinch *v* steal.

pinch, at a in a pinch.

pink *v* knocking in car-engine; **pink gin** gin, bitters & water.

pint *n* this amount of beer, the usual amount served.

pintable *n* game of skill or chance, like bowling but on a table.

pip *n* seed in fleshy fruit; spot on playing cards.

pipe one's eye *coll* weep.

pippin *n* eating apple.

pirn *n Scots* bobbin, spool; fishing reel.

pish interjection used to convey contempt.

piss off *vulg* go away.

pissed *adj vulg* very drunk.

pitch *n* soccer or cricket field.

pitching *n* pavement of cobblestones.

place, give yield.

plaice *n* North Sea fish, the preferred fish with chips.

plane-table *n* drawing board.

plash *n* shallow pool; puddle; **plashy** *adj* wet, marshy.

plaster *n* band-aid.

plat *n* small patch of ground.

plate *n* objects plated with silver or gold, esp electroplated flatware; sterling silverware.

plate-basket *n* basket lined with linen in which forks & spoons are kept.

play at do for pleasure; do half-heartedly; pretend to be; **play hell with** seriously damage or upset; **play to the gallery** *theat* play to audience in those seats for cheap applause.

playing-cards *n* cards.

pleasantry *n* good-natured joke.

pleasure-ground *n* playing field.

pliers *n* pair of pliers.

plimsolls *n* sneakers.

plonk *n coll* cheap or ordinary wine.

ploughman's lunch cheese, bread, pickle & onion.

plug-ugly *n* city hooligan.

plumcake *n* rich cake containing raisins.

plummy *adj* of, like plums; *coll* pleasant and well-paid.

plus fours *n* knickers.

plushy *adj sl* rich, grand; lavish.

po *n coll* chamberpot.

pocket billiards game of pool.

pocketbook *n* wallet.

point *n* electrical wall socket or plug; **in point of fact** in reality; **point steak** best rump (sirloin); **point-duty** *n* duty of policeman stationed at a fixed point.

poke *n* small sack, bag; **poke about** meddle; rummage.

pokerwork *n* ornamentation on wood that is burned in.

poky *adj* cramped.

poleaxed *v* stunned.

pollywog *n* tadpole.

poltroon *n* wretched coward.

pommy *adj, n Aust sl* Englishman.

ponce *n sl* man who protects a prostitute; pimp.

pongo *n* soldier; marine.

pontoon *n* barge; black-jack (card game).

poof *n sl* male homosexual; hassock.

pools *n* weekly soccer betting pool.

poop *n sl* fool.

poor-spirited *adj* cowardly.

poppet *n coll* little darling; pretty child.

pop-shop *n sl* pawnshop.

popsy *n coll* girl; cute girl; jerk.

porch *n* roofed approach to a doorway; vestibule.

porkpie *n* covered pie of chopped pork.

porridge *n* hot cereal; *sl* jail sentence.

porter *n* doorkeeper of hotel, college, public building; dark brown beer.

portress *n* woman doorkeeper, porter.

posset *n* drink of hot milk with ale, wine, spices.

post *n* post office; building for collecting mail; *v* mail a letter; **postal code** zip code; **postbox** *n* mailbox.

postponement *n* rain check.

post restante *n Fr* general delivery.

pot *v* preserve in sealed jars; **potboy** *n* youth employed in a pub to serve beer; **potman** *n* a serving man employed in a public house.

pother *n coll* fuss, uproar.

potholing *n* sport of rock-climbing and cave exploring.

potter away *v* putter away, waste time.

potty *adj coll* easy; made; small, insignificant.

potwalloper *n* (historic) a man who qualified as a householder, and thereby a voter, by virtue of ownership of his own fireplace at which to boil pots; *sl* hearty boozer.

pound *n* basic English monetary unit; **pound along** walk or work hard.

powder and shot, not worth unimportant.

powerpoint *n* wall socket.

pram *n coll abbr* perambulator; baby-carriage; flat-bottomed Dutch lighter (landing-barge).

prank *v* adorn gaudily; dress oneself up; be costumed.

prat *n sl* buttocks; **prattler** *n* chatterer; noisy child.

prawn *n* large shrimp.

preachy *adj coll* inclined to moralize and admonish.

precinct *n* enclosed grounds around a cathedral, monastery, street or paved area excluding traffic; suburbia.

prefect *n* senior pupil with authority over others in school.

premium *n* fee paid for tutoring.

Prerogative, Royal right of a Sovereign to act independently of Parliament.

presently *adv* soon; after a short time.

press on hasten forward; continue despite hardship.

press-stud *n* snap (for clothing)

press-up *n* push-up.

pretty-pretty *adj* merely pretty; affectedly charming.

pricey *adj coll* expensive.

priest *n* club for killing fish.

priggery *n* priggishness; affected moral superiority.

Prime Minister chief minister of the government, akin to the President.

Prince Consort husband of Queen of England.

Prince of Wales heir apparent to the throne.

principal boy woman acting role of hero in pantomime.

prink *v* adorn, make-up, dress up.

prise *v* to open; pry open.

private means unearned income.

private member member of Parliament who is not in the government; **private soldier** enlisted man.

Privy Council council of advisers chosen by the Sovereign.

privy parts external sex organs.

privy seal seal affixed to documents, grants which do not require the great seal.

proceed against to sue, take legal action against.

prom *n coll abbr* promenade concert; embankment; sidewalk.

proper *adv* very; awfully; **proper poorly** quite ill or infirmed.

proprietor *n* owner, esp of a business, store, establishment.

prosily *adv* in a prosy, verbose way.

prosy *adj* dull, uninteresting; long winded.

provost *n* head of certain university colleges; dean *Scots* chief magistrate of a burgh.

prudery *n* outlook or behavior of a prude.

pseud *n sl* person who makes spurious claims to wisdom, taste, etc.

pshaw *interj* rubbish, nonsense.

pub *n coll abbr* **public-house,** tavern.

public school private school, paying boarding school.

publican *n* barkeeper, owner of a pub.

pud *n coll* pudding.

pudding *n* boiled or baked mixture of flour, suet.

puff-paste *n* rich light flaky pastry; napoleon.

pukka *adj* genuine; first-rate; **pukka sahib** true gentleman.

pull about handle roughly; **pull apart** tear apart, break down; **pull down** weaken in health, idea; **pull-in** *n* halting-place; roadside cafe; rest stop; trucker's stop; **pull-on** *n,* corset; **pull round** recover; **pull to pieces** analyze to death, criticize severely.

punch-up *n sl* fist-fight.

puncture *n* flat tire.

punnet *n* small fruit basket.

punt *n* flat-bottomed shallow boat with square ends, propelled by a long pole thrust against the bed of a river or pond; *v* to propel a punt.

punter *n* horse bettor.

pup, be sold a be swindled over a bargain.

puppet, glove hand puppet.

Purbeck *n* fine variety of limestone.

purl *n* mixture of hot beer and gin.

purse-proud *adj* ostentatious about one's riches; nouveau riche.

push off shove off, leave; **pushchair** stroller.

purse *n* change purse; **pursiness** *n* short of breath; **pursy**.

pushball *n* team game played with a ball six feet in diameter.

push-basket *n* shopping cart.

put about spread (rumour); vex, worry; steer on a different course; **put back** replace; retard; check; **put in** insert, interpose, do; present, submit; anchor, moor; **put on** give information about; help to find or communicate with; **put the stopper on** *coll* suppress, check; **put the icing on the pop** it couldn't be worse; **put through** link by telephone with another; cause to undergo; **put wise** make aware; **put down** put to sleep (animals).

pyjamas *n* pajamas.

Q

quad *n* quadrangle (as at Oxford).

quaff *v* drink in large gulps.

quaggy *adj* boggy.

quantity surveyor building cost-estimator.

quay (kee) *n* landing-place; pier; wharf; embankment.

Queen Anne style of furnishings of the early 18th century.

queen cake *n* small soft raisin cake.

queer, in *sl* in trouble; *v* spoil; not well.

queer street financial difficulties; dishonest dealings.

queue *n* line of people or vehicles waiting; **queue up** form a line.

quid *n* pound sterling; piece of chewing tobacco.

quieten *v* calm down, make quiet; become quiet.

quit *v* abandon, leave; depart from; cease, give up, desist; *adj* released from obligation, free.

R

rabbity *adj coll* petty, of little value.

race-course *n* race track.

rachmanism *n* intimidation of tenants.

rackety *adj* disorderly.

raffish *adj* disreputable; dissipated.

rag *v* tease; **rag trade** garment business.

ragday *n* day on which students annually hold a procession with jokes and roudiness, usu in aid of charity.

raglan *adj* sleeves with soft shoulders after Lord Raglan.

ragman *n* ragpicker, scavenger.

raillery *n* banter; good-humored pleasantry.

railway *n* railroad; **railway carriage** coach; **railway guard** conductor.

rake *n* dissolute or immoral man.

rakish *adj* debauched, depraved.

ramp *n* bump in road.

randy *adj Scots* rowdy; *coll* lustful.

rap *n* counterfeit Irish halfpenny; something of no value; **don't care a rap** don't give a damn; **not worth a rap** worthless.

rapecake *n* sheep's food.

rasher (of bacon) *n* slice.

ratable *adj* property valued for taxation.

rates *n* property taxes.

rat-tail *adj* design of flatware.

rattling *adj* excellent, lively.

rave-up *n coll* wild or enthusiastic gathering; session of pop music.

rawly *adv* in a raw, tough way.

reach-me-downs *n* ready-made clothes.

reader *n* university teacher ranking between professor and lecturer.

ready, make prepare.

reception *n* front desk; **receptionist** desk clerk.

recommendable *adj* can be, or deserves to be, recommended.
red admiral *n* black butterfly with red bands.
red ensign flag of British merchant navy.
Red Indian American Indian.
redbrick *adj* university or college founded in modern times; almost any other than Cambridge and Oxford.
redcap *n* military policeman.
redundancy *n* lay-off.
reefer *n* short thick double-breasted coat.
reefknot *n* square knot.
reeky *adj* smoky; dirty.
reel *n* lively Scottish dance.
reel, off the without pause.
referee *n* umpire.
refractor *n* telescope.
Regency *n* of period 1810-20.
Regina *n* official title of a reigning queen.
remainder *n* that which is left; the rest; unsold article offered at reduced price.
Remembrance Day our Veterans Day, around Nov. 11.
remittance *n* bill; allowance.
removal *n* act of shifting one's possessions to a new house; moving.
repertory *n* theater in which many plays are performed successively, each for a short run.
repousse *adj* embossed by hammering from behind.
reserve, without frankly; without restrictions.
retire *v* withdraw, leave; retreat.
return *n* round-trip (ticket).
reverse *n* set back, setback (financial); loss.
reverse charges call collect.
reversing lights back-up lights.
reviewer *n* critic.
Rex *n* title of reigning king; a breed of curly-coated cat.
Reynard *n* traditional name for fox.
rheumy *adj* snotty.

rhubarb *n* hubbub; noisy argument.

ribandry *n* coarse joking; dirty jokes.

ribbon *n* badge of a club, team, order of knighthood; **ribbon development** row-housing.

rice-paper *n* edible paper used for packing candy, cakes.

rick *n* wrench, sprain.

ride for a fall behave recklessly; court disaster; **ride hell for leather** speed all-out; **ride to death** overdo; make dull by repetition.

riesling *n* a dry white Austrian wine.

right *exclam* well! okay; now then; **right you are** I agree; **right sort** socially acceptable chap; **right in the head** sane; **bit of all right** something, someone very nice; **put to rights, put right** straighten out.

rightly *adv* justly, fairly; honestly.

rigorist *n* one who is very strict.

rimy *adj* covered with frost.

ring off end telephone call; **ring up** to telephone, to call.

ring-road *n* circular by-pass road of a city; beltway.

riot, run behave dreadfully.

rip *n* worn-out horse; rake; **ripping** *adj* excellent.

ripely *adv* indecently; drunken; amusing.

rise *n* increase in wages; raise.

road, rules of the traffic laws.

roadhouse *n* country inn or restaurant.

roadster *n* convertible car.

roasting-jack *n* broiling spit.

rock *n* dogfish.

rocker *n* tough, rowdy youth, dressed usu in leather jacket and riding a motorcycle.

rococo *n* lavish 17th and 18th century ornamental style in interior decor based on moorish curves.

rogue *n* criminal; rascal.

roguery *n* dishonesty; mischief.

roller-coaster *n* switchback railway.

roller-towel *n* paper towel.

rollmop *n* rolled pickled herring fillet.

rollneck *n* turtle neck.

rolls, be struck off the be disbarred.

romancer *n* one who composes romances; exaggerator, liar.

Romany *n* gypsy; the gypsy language.

Romish *adj* of or like the Roman Catholic Church.

romp home easy win.

rook *n* gregarious crow.

roost about rummage, pick through rubbish; search for.

rootle *v* dig about, burrow.

rope-end *n* short piece of rope used for whipping, flogging.

ropey *adj* worn-out; old fashioned; inferior.

rorty *adj sl* in good spirits; cheerful.

rose, under the secretly; in confidence.

rota *n* duty roster.

rotovator *n* rototiller.

rotter *n sl* untrustworthy or worthless person; cad.

rouge-et-noir *n Fr* a gambling card-game.

rough diamond uneducated, ill-mannered but good-natured worthy person.

rough-up *n sl* violent fight.

roulette, Vatican *coll* use of 'safe period' as contraceptive method.

round *adj* around; **go the rounds** visit successively; patrol, inspect; **roundabout** *n* traffic circle; **round on** attack suddenly; turn against; **round the bend** *sl* mad; crazy.

rounders *n* team-game played with bat and ball, like baseball.

round-house *n* prison.

roundsman *n* door-to-door salesman or delivery servant.

row (row) *n coll* noisy disturbance; brawl.

rowdyism *n* rowdy behavior.

rowing-boat *n* rowboat; **rowlock** *n* oarlock.

royal *adj* of, like or befitting the sovereign; size of paper.

rozzer *n sl* policeman.

rubber *n* eraser.

rubbish *n* waste paper, trash, refuse; anything worthless; nonsense.

rubbishly *adj* worthless, useless; nonsensical.

rubdown *n* massage.

rub up *v* refresh one's memory.

ruck *n* pile; crowd; horses left behind.

rucksack *n* back-pack.

ruddy *adj* glowing red; *sl* unpleasant, extreme (*euph* for **bloody**).

ruffian *n* violent person tending towards crime.

rug *n* car blanket; bedspread.

Rugby *n* game like both soccer and football; **rugger** *n coll* rugby; one who plays rugby.

rum *adj coll* strange, queer, odd.

rumble *v* see through; comprehend.

rumly *adv coll* queerly; oddly.

rumpsteak *n* steak near the rump; *usu* on the menu as sirloin.

run at hurl oneself at; attack; **run down** pursue and catch; search for; **run high** be intense; **run in** drive at moderate speed (esp car) when new.

rune *n* incomprehensible writing.

running lights parking lights.

run up hoist rapidly; make or build hastily.

Ruritanian *adj* full of melodramatic adventures, plots, intrigues.

rushy *adj* abounding in weeds, rushes.

rusty, turn become difficult to manage, turn nasty.

ruth *n* mercy, pity.

ruttish *adj* in a rut; lustful.

S

sabot (sabo) *n* wooden shoe; wood-soled shoe.

sacerdotalism (saser*do*talism) *n* priestly principles or practices.

sack *v coll* dismiss, fire from job; *n* a dry white wine from Spain.

sacking *n* burlap.

saddle of lamb *n* mutton joint cut from animal's back.

safety-razor *n* razor.

St. George's Cross the Greek cross used in the flag of Great Britain.

salad *n* meat, cheese, served cold with lettuce garnish.

salad cream salad dressing, mayonnaise; **salad days** youthful immaturity.

saleroom *n* auction room, house.

sally *n* outburst, sudden rush; unexpectedly rapid and witty remark; **sally forth** rush out; set out; **sally-lunn** *n* hot buttered teacake.

salmagundi *n* dish of chopped meat, etc., seasoned with anchovies.

salmon-trout *n* sea-trout.

salon *n Fr* reception-room; circle of people prominent in the arts.

saloon *n* large room used for receptions; sedan car; **saloon bar** the more comfortable and expensive side of a pub.

salopian *adj* of Shropshire.

salt-beef *n* corned-beef.

saltcellar *n* saltshaker.

salver *n* tray.

sam *n coll* soul.

Sam Browne *n* army officer's belt.

sandboy *n* as happy as a sandboy very happy; **sandglass** *n* hourglass, egg-timer; **sandpit** *n* sand-box.

sandwichman *n* one who carries sandwich boards advertising products.

sangfroid (sng-fwah) *n Fr* imperturbable, calm.

sanitary towel sanitary napkin.

sapless *adj* dry, withered; lifeless.

sap-rot *n* dry-rot.

saratoga *n* large traveling trunk.

sark *n Scots* shirt, nightshirt.

sarking *n* thin boards for lining a roof under the slates; 'sleepers'.

sarky *n* sarcastic.

satchel *n* book-bag.

satin-paper *n* glossy writing-paper.

saucepan *n* small pot.

sausage-dog *n coll* dachshund.

sausage-roll *n* baked pastry containing sausage-meat.

sauterne *n* a light, dry white French wine.

save *prep adv* except.

Savile Row *adj* classy dresser.

savoury *n* any light, tasty dish served as an appetizer.

savoy *n* winter cabbage.

sawney *n* Scotsman; *sl* fool, simpleton.

Saxon *n* one of a Teutonic people from N Germany who conquered England in the 5th & 6th centuries.

saxony *n* fine woolen material.

scallywag *n* rogue, scamp.

scamp *n* rascal, rogue; *v* make or do carelessly; leave unfinished.

scampi *n* dish of large shrimp, usu fried.

scandalmonger *n* gossip.

scapegrace *n* rascal, ne'er-do-well.

scaremonger *n* rumor-spreader.

scarper *v sl* run away, take off.

scat *n* tribute; rent paid to the Crown in Orkney and Shetland.

scatty *adj coll* crazy; cheerfuly scatterbrained.

schedule (*shed*ewl) *n* detailed program of things to be done.

schnapps *n* name for various spirits, esp Hollands gin.

school-leaver *n* drop-out.

schoolmaster *n* teacher.

scissile *adj* that which can be cut.

scobs *n* sawdust; shavings.

scone (skon/skOn) *n* small soft raisin bun; *sl* head.

scot *n* tax; payment.

Scotch *adj* of or from Scotland; **Scotch broth** mutton soup with pear barley; **Scotch egg** hard-boiled egg enclosed with sausage in frie pastry; **Scotch mist** fog mixed with fine drizzling rain.

Scotland Yard London police headquarters.

Scottie *n coll* Scotch terrier; Scotsman.

scoundrel *n* rogue, rascal; blackguard.

scouse *n* thick meat and vegetable broth, typical of Liverpool.

scrag *n* bony end of neck of mutton; anything thin and bony.

scran *n* left-over scraps.

scrannel *adj* thin; feeble; reedy.

scrap *n* fight, brawl; scrappy *adj* fragmentary.

scrape, bow and act obsequiously or too ceremoniously.

scrappy *adj* fragmentary.

screw *n* half-ounce of tobacco; *coll* wages, miser; broken down o diseased horse; *sl* prison warden; **screwed** *adj sl* drunk.

scribbling-pad *n* scratch pad.

scrimshanker *n* one who avoids doing his duty; malingerer.

scrivener *n* one who draws contracts; notary; moneylender.

scrub *n* brushwood, stunted bush or tree.

scrum *n* basic Rugby play in which forwards of both teams strug gle to pick up the ball rolling around between them.

scrumpy *n* rough cider.

scrutineer *n* canvasser, vote-getter.

scullery *n* room where dishes, etc. are washed and other housework done.

scullion *n* dishwasher.

scunner *n coll* a strong dislike.

scupper *v coll* disable, ruin.

scut *n* short tail, esp that of a rabbit.

sea, put to set sail; **at sea** confused, bewildered.

seabank *n* sea-wall; **sea-front** *n* waterfront; **sea-lawyer** *n* one wh is always complaining of injustice (to him) and asserting his right (over others); **sea-mile** *n* nautical mile, 6,080 ft.; **sea-pink** *n* thrift

124

season ticket commutation ticket.

secateurs *n* pruning shears.

secretary *n* writing desk.

sedan *n* covered chair carried by two poles.

see about deal with, attend to; **see after; see to.**

seed, run to dissipate; lose freshness or energy.

seedsman *n* store that sells flowers, seeds, garden equipment, etc.

seeing *conj* considering that.

seemly *adj* proper, decent.

self-absorbed *adj* excessively egotistical; vain.

self-abuse *n* masterbation.

self-acting *adj* automatic.

self-complacent *adj* unduly pleased with oneself.

self-conceit *n* too high an opinion of oneself.

self-contained *adj* with cooking facilities (accommodations).

self-effacement *n* act of avoiding being noticed.

self-feeder *n* machine which refuels itself.

self-forgetful *adj* unselfish.

selfhood *n* individuality; identity.

selfsame *adj* exactly the same.

self-seeker *n* one who pursues his own advantage, regardless of others.

sell *n sl* fraud, hoax, disappointment; **sell off** sell cheaply so as to get rid of; have a sale.

sellotape *n* transparent tape.

semolina *n* cream of wheat.

send down expel from university; **send packing** dismiss rudely, get rid of; **send up** *sl* show as ridiculous or false; *n* parody.

sennight *n* week.

sentrybox *n* small doorless hut to shelter a sentry.

sept *n* Irish or Highland clan or family.

sergeant *n* police officer next in rank above a constable.

serve *v* wait on.

service flats apartment-hotel.

serviette *n* table-napkin, esp a paper one.

serving-man *n* male servant.

set about set out, begin to do; *coll* attack, hit.

set-down *n* rebuke, snub; **set forth** begin a journey; go out; **set i**
settle in; appear and gradually increase; flow; **set right** correct; **se**
to begin vigorously, esp to eat or fight; **set upon** attack.

settee *n* love seat.

setting lotion hair-spray.

settle *n* long wooden high-backed seat.

sewage works waste-treatment plant.

sexton *n* man employed by a church as caretaker, gravediggers.

shabby *adj* pettily dishonest, shameful; **shabby-genteel** *adj* livin
in near-poverty but struggling to conceal the fact.

shade, in the forgotten, overlooked; in the shadow of someone else

shade away disappear or change very gradually.

shadow cabinet leaders of an opposition party who will be expecte
to form the cabinet when they return to power.

shadowy *adj* full of shade; dark; dim; vague; mysterious.

shagreen *n* strong untanned leather made from horsehide, sharkskin

shakedown *n* makeshift bed.

shallop *n* light open dory.

shallow-brained *adj* weak-minded; foolish; superficial.

sham *v* feign, simulate; make a pretence of; *adj* pretended, faked

shambles *n* slaughter-house, butcher's stall or shop; place of utte
confusion.

shambolitic *adj coll* chaotic.

shamrock *n* species of trefoil, the national emblem of Ireland.

shandy, shandygaff *n* mixture of beer and ginger-ale.

Shank's pony, mare walking as a compulsory alternative transport

shape up to stand up to; defy, challenge.

share-pusher *n* one who offers shares in unsound companies.

shares *n* stocks.

sharper *n coll* swindler, cheat, card-shark.

sharp-set *adj* having a keen appetite.

Shavian *adj* of or like Bernard Shaw or his works or times.

shay *n* chaise, sofa.

shearlegs *n* apparatus for hoisting heavy weights; derrick.

sheeny *adj* bright, glossy.

sheep-dip *n* disinfectant for preserving wool or killing vermin on sheep.

sheep-anchor *n* large emergency anchor; chief support; last refuge.

sheila *n Aust coll* girl, woman.

shelf-mark *n* code-mark on book; library number.

shelta *n* secret language of Irish and Welsh tinkers and gypsies.

sheltie, shelty *n* Shetland pony.

shepherd's pie meat and onions baked under a layer of mashed potatoes, esp for pub lunches.

sherbet *n* cooling Oriental drink of water and fruit juices; type of effervescing drink; effervescent powder.

Sheriff, High honorary administrative and judicial official in certain cities and counties.

shieling, shealing *n* hut used by shepherds, sportsmen.

shifter *n theat* stage-hand.

shillelagh *n* cudgel, stick made of oak or blackthorn.

shilling *n* British silver coin worth five new pence.

shimmery *adj* that shimmers; glowing.

shindy *n coll* row, brawl, disturbance.

shine *v* polish; look happy; show great intelligence, wit; be excellent at; **take the shine out of** spoil the newness, or brilliance of; humiliate, put down.

shingle *n* coarse loose pebbles on the beach.

ship-biscuit *n* coarse, hard dry cracker; **ship-broker** *n* forwarding agent, shipper; **ship-chandler** *n* ship and boating supply store.

shippen *n* cowhouse.

ship's-husband *n* shipowner's agent who attends to repairs, provisions, etc.

shire *n* county, territorial division of the British Isles.

Shires, the the Midland counties, in which hunting is esp popular.

shirt, boiled stiffened formal shirt worn with tuxedo; **have one's shirt out** be in a bad temper.

shirty *adj sl* bad-tempered.

shocker *n* one who or that which shocks; sensational story or book or magazine; something of poor quality.

shocking *adj* offensive; scandalous; horrifying, disgusting.

shoes, another pair of quite another matter; **know where the shoe pinches** know the meaning of trouble, poverty, sorrow.

shoeblack *n* shoeshine boy, bootblack.

shog off *sl* get going, beat it.

shoot a line *coll* boast, brag; **shoot the moon** *sl* move out at night to avoid paying the rent; **shoot one's bolt** make one's utmost effort; **be shot of** be rid of.

shooting-brake *n* station wagon.

shooting match, whole everything.

shooting-stick *n* walking-stick whose handle unfolds into a seat.

shop *n* store; *sl* inform against, betray to police.

shop-assistant *n* clerk in a retail store; **shopkeeper** *n* store owner; **shopwalker** *n* floor-walker.

short commons low rations.

shortcake *n* shortbread; flat cake.

shorthand typist stenographer; secretary.

shot, like a very fast; gladly, willingly; **get shot of** get away from; complete.

shout *n coll* a round of drinks.

shout at the floor *coll* throw-up, vomit.

shove off *coll* go away.

show a leg *exclam* get going!

showerbath *n* shower.

showroom *n* large room where goods in stores are displayed.

shunt *n* switch.

shy *v* toss, throw.

sick *v* throw-up; **sick at heart** sad.

sideboard *n* buffet.

side boards *n* sideburns; short whiskers.

side lights parking lights.

sightly *adj* pleasant to look at.

signet *n* a small seal; **signet ring** ring set with a signet.

sign-manual *n* royal signature; autograph book.

silencer *n* muffler.

silk, take become a Queen's Counsel, a public prosecutor.

silly season summer recess of Parliament, a hard-news drought.

silver gilt silver article plated with gold.

sing small *coll* behave humbly.

single-hearted *adj* honest, sincere; devoted; **single** (ticket) *n* one-way; **singlet** *n* man's undershirt.

singsong *n* session of cheerful, unrehearsed singing.

Sinn Fein (shin-*fayn*) *n* Irish nationalist and republican movement.

sippet *n* small piece of toast or fried bread used as a garnish.

sir *n* term of formal address to a man, titled knight or baronet.

sit-in *n* protest against social or political injustice by occupying a public building until thrown out by force.

sixes & sevens in a tizzy.

sixth form highest grade in secondary (high) school.

skep *n* wicker or straw basket; beehive.

skerry *n* rocky isle; reef.

sketch *coll* ridiculous person.

skew, on the aslant, crooked.

skidlid *n coll* cyclist's helmet.

skiffle-group *n* group of musicians using guitar and improvised percussion instruments.

skilly *n* thin broth or gruel.

skinned, keep one's eyes be on the look-out.

skinhead *n* violent young hooligan with close-cropped hair.

skint *n* penniless person.

skip *n* trash container; **skipper** *v sl* sleep in the open air.

skipper *v sl* sleep in the open air.

skipping-rope *n* jump rope.

skirting board baseboard.

skittles *n* ninepins; game played with these; *coll* nonsense.

skive *v* avoid work, shirk.

skivvy *n sl* domestic maid, esp maid of all work.

Skye-terrier small rough-haired Scotch terrier.

skypilot *n sl* clergyman.

skyscape *n* picture or view consisting mainly of sky.

slanging match exchange of insults, violent verbal quarrel.

slapbang *adv coll* suddenly; roughly; **slapdash** *adv* carelessly; rashly; *adj* slipshod; **slap-up** *adj coll* lavish, first-class.

slashing *adj coll* excellent, lovely.

slate *v coll* criticize harshly; thrash; **slating** *n coll* severe reprimand.

sledge *n* sled, sleigh.

sleeping-car *n* pullman; **sleeping-draught** *n* pill; **sleeping-partner** *n* silent partner; **sleeping-policeman** *n* temporary traffic lights.

sleevelink *n* cufflink, stud.

sleight *n* dexterous trick.

slimming *n* reducing.

sling one's hook *coll* go away.

sling out forcibly drive out.

Sloane ranger socialite.

slip *n* bathing suit.

slipper *n* lady's light evening shoe; **slipper-slopper** *adj* sentimental.

slippy *adj coll* slippery; quick.

sliproad *n* minor bypass road; **slipway** *n* launching slip.

slob *n* muddy ground.

sloe *n* wild fruit of black horn; **sloe gin** liqueur of gin in which sloes have been steeped.

slogger *n* one who hits hard; hard worker, plodder.

slops *n* loose working clothes; readymade clothes.

slosh *n sl* foolish sentimentality.

slough-hat *n* hat with large brim down at one side.

slowcoach *n* dull, old-fashioned person.

slug *v* lie lazily in bed; **sluggard** *n* habitually lazy person.

sluttish *adj* idle and untidy; secretly.

smack *n* small fishing boat; have a smack at; *coll* try; **smack in the eye** rebuff, insult.

small beer weak beer; something trivial.

smallholding *n* small farm rented by a county council; small farm.

smalls *n* underwear.

smarmy *adj coll* flattering, insincerely polite.

smash and grab raid robbery by breaking and entering.

smasher *n coll* remarkable person or thing; **smashing** *adj* outstanding, delightful.

smear-word *n* scandalous epithet; innuendo.

smoke, the London.

smokeless zone where burning coal is forbidden; London, Manchester, etc.

smooch *v* dawdle, hang around.

smooth-faced *adj* without a beard; having a flattering expression; insincere, glib.

smoothing-iron *n* iron for pressing clothes.

smorbrod *n* Danish cold appetizers served on small pieces of bread.

smugly *adv* in a smug way.

smutty *adj* obscene, smuttily.

snap *n* "spit" (children's game).

snappish *adj* giving sharp replies; irritable.

snarky *adj coll* bad-tempered.

snick *v* cut slightly, nick.

snidy *adj sl* crafty; knowing.

snip *n coll* profitable bargain; tailor.

snog *v sl* kiss and caress, pet; *n* petting session.

snorty *adj coll* annoyed, disapproving.

snowslip *n* avalanche.

snuggery *n* small, warm comfortable room.

soak *n* act of soaking; taking a bath; heavy downpour; long period of hard drinking.

sod *n vulg sl* sodomite; unpleasant, vindictive or ill-tempered person; fellow, person, chap; **sod it** screw it!

softy *n coll* silly sentimental person; imbecile; coward.

solder (solder) *n* soft alloy for joining metals.

sold on *coll* convinced of the merits of.

solo *n* two-handed whist.

soke *n* early English privilege of holding court usu connected with feudal rights of lordship.

solicitor *n* lawyer.

something *n coll* excellent, considerable.

song *n coll* trifle; **make a song about** *coll* make a fuss over.

sonsy *adj Scots* good-looking; buxom; good-natured.

soppy *adj* thoroughly wet; *coll* silly, sentimental.

sorbet *n* sherbet.

sorry *adj* miserable, worthless.

sort, good *coll* likeable person; **sort you out** help you out; organize things.

sot *n* habitual drunkard; fuddled person; **sottish.**

souchong *n* kind of China tea.

sound *adj* logical, justifiable; prudent, reliable; thorough; **soundbox** *n* amplifier; **soundly** *adv* thoroughly; healthily; firmly; well.

soup, in the *sl* in difficultiees, in trouble.

soup-plate *n* soup bowl.

sourly *adv* gloomy, bitter.

souse *n* pickle; anything preserved in brine.

southron *adj, n Scots* of or an Englishman.

sovereign *n* supreme ruler, monarch; British gold coin nominally worth one pound sterling.

sozzled *adj coll* drunk, befuddled.

spado *n* castrated man, eunuch; impotent fellow.

Spanish Main Caribbean Sea.

spanker *n* fast horse; *coll* fine specimen.

spanking *adj coll* brisk, quick-moving; great, large; fine.

spanner *n* wrench (fixed jaw); **spanner in the works** *coll* deliberate hindrance, sabotage.

spares *n* spare-parts, extras; provisions; stock.

spark *n* gay young blade; **sparking-plug** *n* sparkplug; **sparkler** *n sl* diamond.

spatula *n* tongue-depressor; kitchen tool.

Special Branch wing of Scotland Yard for political crimes.

special constable person temporarily sworn as a policeman.

special pleading *coll* quibbling, unfair argument.

specimen *n coll* odd person.

speech-day *n* annual prize-giving day at a school.

speech-reading *n* lip-reading.

132

speedcop *n sl* traffic policeman; **speed-merchant** *n sl* fast driver.

speller *n* spelling book.

spencer *n* short woolen jacket.

spend a penny visit the bathroom.

spieler *n sl* card-shark; swindler.

spiffing *adj sl* fine, delightful.

spifflicate *v sl* smash, crush.

spigot *n* peg or plug in barrel.

spiky *adj* quickly take offense; *sl* holding High Church views.

spillikins *n* "Pick up Sticks".

spineless *adj* gutless, yellow.

spinney *n* small copse or wood.

spindleshanks *n* person with long thin legs.

spin out *coll* make a story or yarn longer than it need be; **flat spin** *coll* panic.

spiny *adj* covered with, full of spines; perplexing, difficult.

spirit-lamp *n* alcohol lamp.

spirit-level *n* level with alcohol instead of water.

spirits *n* alcoholic beverages, esp whiskey, gin, etc.

spiry *adj* like a spire, tall.

spit *n* depth of earth equal to that of a spade's blade; **dead spit of** the spitting image of.

spiv *n sl* shifty guy.

splash *n coll* prominent display.

splat *n* horizontal bar in chair-back.

spode *n* type of porcelain.

spoiling for eagerly seeking.

sponge bag make-up bag.

sponsored walk form of charitable fund-raising.

sporran *n* Highlander's pouch worn in front of a kilt.

sportscar *n* two-seater sportcar; **sports-jacket** *n* sport-coat.

spot *n* small quantity; **spot-on** *adj coll* perfectly aimed, done.

spout, down the *sl* lost, ruined; **up the spout** *sl* spawned; pregnant.

sprat *n* tiny fish, like herring.

springback *n* loose-leaf book.

spud *n* spade; *sl* friend; *coll* potato; **spud-bashing** *n sl* peeling potatoes.

spunk *n* tinder, touchwood; *coll* courage; hot temper.

spyhole *n* peephole.

spy out explore or discover secretly.

squab-pie *n* pigeon-pie; mutton pie with onions and apples.

squails *n* tiddly-winks.

square away prepare, make ready.

square-bashing *n sl* military drill.

square-one *n* starting point; **get square with** *coll* revenge on, achieve equally with; **square the circle** attempt the impossible.

squash *n* drink made of fruit syrup and water.

squeak, narrow narrow escape.

squeezer *n* one or that which squeezes.

squib *n* sparkler; pointed remark that fails to achieve its goal.

squidge *v* squeeze, squash.

squiffy *adj* tipsy, inebriated.

squiggly *adj* twisted, wriggly.

squint-eyed *adj* squinting.

squire *n* country (or landed) gentleman; *coll* boss; **squirearchy** country landowners as a class.

squireen *n* pretty squire, esp in Ireland.

squit *n sl* unimportant person; worthless rubbish.

squitters *n sl* diarrhea.

stackpipe *n* drainpipe; the main sewer line of a house.

stager, old old hand; old ham.

stagy *adj* consciously dramatic, over-emphatic.

stalking-horse *n* that which conceals one's hostile intentions.

stall *n* look-out for thief.

stalls *n* theater seats in the orchestra.

stand *v* threat; pay fox; **stand down** withdraw from contest, election; **stand with** support, ally oneself with.

standard-lamp *n* standing lamp.

starkers *adj sl* stark-naked.

starts, by fits and jerkily, spasmodically.

state-carriage *n* carriage in ceremonial occasions.

state school public school.

step-ins *n* garments or shoes that can be slipped into or on.

sterling *adj* in British money; **Sterling Area** group of countries whose currencies are tied to British monetary standards.

stern-sheets *n* space and benches at rear of boat; cockpit.

steward *n* catering manager of college.

stick *n* reserved or dull person; **wrong end of the stick** misunderstanding; **stick up to** face boldly; stand up to.

sticker *n coll* perseverant worker.

sticking-plaster *n* band-aid; adhesive tape.

stickjaw *adj sl* glutinous taffy, chewing-gum, etc.

sticky *adj* awkward; *sl* unpleasant, painful; **sticky wicket** delicate situation.

stilly *adv* quietly, calmly.

stilton *n* variety of rich cheese.

stinker *n* difficult task or problem.

stinks *n sl* chemistry.

stirrabout *n* kind of porridge, oatmeal.

stirrup-cup *n* cup of wine or brandy drunk on horseback before a hunt.

stiver *n* small coin; trifling sum.

stocking *n* knitted or woven long sock.

stockist *n* supplier; wholesaler.

stock-will *adv* motionless.

stock-taking *n* inventory.

stodge *n coll* heavy and unappetizing food; *v* cram oneself with food.

stoep (stoop) *v* veranda, porch.

stomach *v* digest; eat with relish; put up with.

stone *n* pit (fruit); (weight) fourteen pounds; **stone-axe** *n* stone-cutter's hammer; **stone's-cast** *n* a stone's throw; **stone the crows** exclamation of surprise; **stony** *adj sl* penniless.

stopcock *n* valve or tap for stopping or regulating flow.

stopple *n* stopper, bung, plug.

stores *n* equipment; ammunition; supplies; stock.

stormy petrel type of bird believed to portend storms.

stout *n* strong dark beer.

straight away; straight off; straightway immediately; **straight on** straight ahead.

strait-waistcoat *n* straitjacket.

strand *n* shore, beach; boardwalk.

strapping *adj* tall, strong, muscular.

street *n* paved road with houses on both sides; **not in the same street with** not to be compared with; much inferior to; **streets ahead of** very far ahead of; **up one's street** up one's alley.

strewth it's the truth.

strine *n coll* Australian English.

stroke *n* slash /.

strongroom *n* vault.

stroppy *adj coll* bad-tempered; aggressive.

Stuart *n* member of the royal family that rules in Scotland 1374-1714 and England 1603-1714.

stuffed, get drop dead.

stumer *n sl* worthless check; forged note.

stumps, stir one's *coll* hurry, become more active.

stunner *n* attractive person.

sub-editor *n* assistant editor.

subs *n* dues; subscriptions.

subway *n* tunnel, underground passage by which pedestrians can cross beneath a railway, road.

suchlike *adj* of such a kind.

sugar-soap *n* paint remover.

suiting *n* cloth to be made into suits.

sulks *n* mood of sullenness or ill-humor.

sultana *n coll* raisin.

summat *n coll dial* something.

sump *n* oil-pan, reservoir for lubricating oil in car.

sums *n* addition.

sunblind *n* blind, shade for a window.

sun-lounge *n* sun room, conservatory.

sunshade *n* parasol, umbrella for the sun.

sun-up *n* sunrise.

super *adj* marvelous, great.

superintendent *n* police officer ranking above chief inspector.

superannuate *v* pension off.

supertax *n* additional income tax for those with large incomes.

supremo *n coll* dictator; commander; the boss.

supply *n* temporary servant or teacher.

surgery *n* doctor's office, consulting room or dispensary.

surgical spirit rubbing alcohol.

surrounds *n* uncovered floor at edges of carpet.

suspender-belt *n* woman's girdle.

suss-out *v sl* detect; suspect, discover.

swag *n sl Aust* pack, bundle; **swag-bellied** *adj* having a large floppy belly.

swagger-cane *n* soldier's short walking-stick.

swagman *n Aust* vagrant, tramp; itinerant laborer; peddler.

swanning, swan about, swan around *v coll* move slowly and majestically; wander about, travel aimlessly without destination.

swanskin *n* very soft flannel.

swatter *n* fly-swatter.

swede *n* turnip; rutabaga.

sweep *n* man who cleans soot from chimneys; **sweep the board** take all the winnings.

sweet *n* dessert.

sweeting *n* sweet apple.

sweetmeat *n* chocolate candy.

sweet-oil *n* olive oil; salad oil.

sweets *n* candy; **sweet-shop** *n* candy store.

swimming-bath *n* swimming pool, usu enclosed; **swimming-belt** *n* water-wings.

swimmingly *adv* wonderfully.

swimsuit *n* bathing suit.

swing the lead avoid work by false excuses.

swingeing *adj* forceful; huge.

swish *adj* smart, elegant.

Swiss bun iced cruller, danish; **Swiss roll** jelly-roll.

switched on *coll* up-to-date, trendy.

swiz *n coll* bitter disappointment; deception; fraud.

swizzle *n coll* swindle; disappointment; a mixed drink; stick for taking the bubbles out of champagne.

swollen-headed *adj* conceited, swell-headed.

swot *v coll* study hard; **swot up** make great efforts to learn or memorize; bone up; **swot** *n coll* who hits the books hard.

T

ta *interj coll* thank you.

tabard *n* sleeveless coat worn by heralds.

tabby *n* spiteful gossiping woman.

table *v* put up for discussion.

tablet *n* pill.

tabloid *n* newspaper presenting facts in simplified form.

Taffy *n coll* Welshman.

tag around with *coll* be constant companion of.

tail-lamp *n* tail-light.

tailor *n* who makes outer clothing, esp for men; clothing store.

take for believe to be; **take hold** grasp; acquire power over; **take in** comprise; admit to one's home; receive; deceive; impose on; make narrower; **take into one's head** suddenly think or decide; **take-away** *n, adj coll* take-out; to go; **take-up** *n* draw together; join, start.

talk round discuss without reaching any conclusion.

talking-to *n coll* scolding, reprimand.

tallboy *n* tall chest of drawers; high-boy.

tallow-chandler *n* candlemaker; candleseller.

tallyman *n* salesman who sells goods on installment; **tally-shop** *n* where goods are sold on installment.

tameless *adj* wild, untamable; **tamely** *adv* in a tame way; passively.

tammy *n coll* tam-o'-shanter, a broad woolen beret.

tank up fill up the tank of.

tanning *n sl* beating, shipping.

tannoy *n* loudspeaker; bull-horn.

tap *n* faucet, spigot.

taproom *n* room in pub where barrels are stored and where cheaper drinks are sold.

tariff-wall *n* setting high duties on imports to discourage them.

tar-macadam *n* tarmac, paved road.

tarn *n* small lake on moor or among mountains.

tart *n* pie; **tartlet** *n* small tart; **tart up** dress up.

tartan *n* woollen fabric with various coloured checks forming patterns belonging to each Highland clan (old family); garment made of this.

tarted up overdressed; gaudy; vulgar.

tartly *adv* sharply, acidly.

tartuffe *n* religious hypocrite.

tarty *adj sl* of or like a prostitute.

task, take to reprove, find fault with.

tassie *n* goblet, beaker, mug.

tat *n* bricabrac; old clothes, ornaments etc. of little value.

tatto *n* military pageant and parade, esp performed by night as entertainment; **the devil's tattoo** drumming fingers on table.

tatty *adj* untidy; shabby; run-down.

taw *n* a marble; game of marbles.

tawse *n Scots* leather strap.

taxi-rank *n* taxi stand, line.

tea *n* national quiet pastime of Britons, beginning with tea on rising out of bed; elevenses, afternoon & high teas.

tea-caddy *n* container or can for tea leaves; **tea-cosy** *n* thick cloth cover for keeping a teapot warm; **tea-kettle** *n* water-kettle; **tea leaf** *sl* thief; **teapoy** *n* small three-legged table; **tea-trolley** *n* tea cart.

tearaway *n sl* violent young hooligan.

tearing *adj coll* furious, rushing.

teaser *n* problem

tea-things *n* crockery, china, silverware for serving tea.

teatime *adj, n* of or at the usual time for afternoon tea (3-5 p.m.).

tec *n sl abbr* detective; technical college.

technicolor yawn vomit.

teddy-boy *n* type of tough youth with fastidious taste in Edwardian dress; **Teddy suit** black suit with narrow trousers (pants).

telephonist *n* operator; receptionist.

telling *adj* very effective, impressive.

telltale *n* one who gives away secrets; gossip; informer.

telly *n, coll abbr* television.

tenement *n* one of some rooms in a house, each rented by a family.

tenpins *n* bowling.

tenter *n* one who looks after machinery; **tent-pegging** *n* cavalry sport of trying to carry off on a lance a tent-peg in the ground.

terminal *n* railroad station.

terminus *n* terminal (end).

terrace *n* row houses; open stands in stadium, bleachers.

territorials *n* National Guard; home guard.

terry *n* toweling.

Terylene *n* polyester fiber; cloth made of polyester.

test match one of a series of cricket matches; play-off.

tester *n* canopy over a bed.

tetchy, techy *adj* easily irritated, touchy.

thankee *interj coll* thank you.

thatching *n* covering a roof with thatch; materials for thatching.

theatre *n* operating room in a hospital.

theatricals *n* dramatic performances by amateurs.

thence *adv* from that place; from that time; for that reason.

thenceforward *adv* from that time onward.

there you are! *interj* here's what you wanted; so there! **not all there** mentally deficient; **there you go** you're doing it again.

thereinafter *adv* later in the same document.

thereon *adv* on this or that.

thereupon *adv* in consequence of this or that.

thewy *adj* muscular.

thick, a bit too much to put up with.

thickish *adv* in a thick way; **thickly.**

thievish *adj* of or like a thief.

thimblerigging *n* swindling game, like the shell game, only with a pea under one of three thimbles; trickery, cheating, etc.

thin *adj* inadequate; **thin on the ground** rare, not easily available; **a thin time** *coll* an unpleasant, miserable time; **thin red line** *coll* the last (thank goodness) people to leave from a party, gathering.

141

thing, just the just what was wanted; **know a thing or two** be no fool; be experienced; **not the thing** socially incorrect.

thingummy *n coll* person or thing, the name of whom or which has been forgotten; whatsisname.

thinkable *adj* capable of being thought; reasonable.

think-piece *n coll* article or essay seriously analyzing a problem.

this, what's all? what's the trouble, disturbance, here?

thisness *n* individuality; thick with the quality of this.

thorny *adj* troublesome; prickly; causing problems.

thorough-going *adj* uncompromising; going to any length; complete.

thorp, thorpe *n* small village.

thrash about move limbs violently; be in disorder.

three-decker *n* old type of sailing ship with three decks; pulpit with three tiers; club-sandwich; three-volume novel; **three-seater** *n* long couch .

threeply *adj* having three strands, esp wool; three layers.

thrice *adv* three times.

through *conj* connected (telephone).

throughway *n* road with no stopping; highway.

throw about toss; wave violently; scatter.

throw off remove hurriedly; recover from; utter easily; **throw oneself at** rush violently towards; make undignified attempts to win the love of; **throw open** open wide; allow general access to; **throw up** give up, lose interest in; **throw up the sponge** toss in the towel; surrender; **throw-out** *n* one who or that which has been rejected, discarded.

thrust, cut and exchange of sword blows, repartee, rapid argument.

thruster *n* one who ruthlessly sets out to succeed; one who rides too close to the hounds at hunt.

thug *n* murderous raffian, gangster; **thuggery** *n* brutal violence.

thumb a lift hitch-hike.

thumbs up! exclamation of triumph, success, approval.

thumbed *adj* soiled by handling; fingered.

thumbnut *n* wing-nut.

thumping *adj coll* very big or remarkable.

thundery *adj* of or like thunder; menacingly, angrily.

thwack *v* strike vigorously.

tich *n sl* nickname for a small man.

tick *n coll* credit; check-mark; **tick off** *sl* rebuke sharply, scold; **tick over** engine running quietly in neutral; be inactive.

tick-tack *n* system of gestures of bookmakers.

tiddler *n* very small fish.

tiddley *adj sl* slightly drunk, tipsy; *naut* trim, spruced up.

tidy *adj* arranged neatly and in order; *n* small box, bag; **tidy up** make neat, clean, orderly.

tied-house *n* pub bound to a brewery for its supplies.

tiffin *n* light lunch.

tights *n* panty hose.

tike, tyke *n* dog, cur; ill-bred person, boor; Yorkshireman.

tilt *n* canvas hood or cover; awning.

time, all in good soon enough, no need for haste; **have no time for** detest, despise; **time, gentleman!** publican's cry for last drinks.

timepiece *n* clock, watch.

timeserver *n* toady; one who unscrupulously alters his opinions to please those in power.

time table *n* schedule (trains, etc.)

timeworn *adj* old; showing signs of wear or decay.

tin *n* can, esp canned foods; **put the tin hat (lid) on** bring to an abrupt or unpleasant climax; **tin** *v* preserve; put in cans.

tinker *n* one who mends pots, pans; gypsy, tramp.

tinkle *v coll* call on the telephone; *n* telephone call.

tin-opener *n* can-opener.

tinned *adj* canned (food).

tinpot *adj* made of inferior materials; petty, worthless.

tip *n* dump; trash heap; **tip the wink** to inform privately, give a hint to; **tipcart** *n* wheel-barrow; **tipcat** *n* game in which a piece of wood is hit with a stick.

tippet *n* fur worn over neck and shoulders; stole; cape.

tipple *n coll* strong drink.

topsy-cake *n* sponge-cake soaked in wine and served with custard.

tit *n* small bird; titmouse; *sl* ineffectual fool, weakling.

titbit *n* small bit of tasty food; interesting bit of gossip; tidbit.

titch *n coll* small person; **titchy** *adj* tiny,, contemptible.

titfer *n sl* a hat; tit-fer-tat.

tittle *n* jot, very small particle; **tittle-tattle** *n* gossip; tattle-tale.

T-junction *n* T (roads).

toad-in-the-hole *n* meat, usu sausage, cooked in batter.

toady *n* fawning flatterer; *v* fawn upon.

toastrack *n* stand which holds slices of toast separately.

tobacconist *n* cigar store.

toby-jug *n* mug shaped like an old man with three-cornered hat.

tod *n sl* on one's tod alone.

toff *n sl* rich, upper-class, or well-dressed man; a swell.

toffee *n* taffy; **toffee-nosed** *adj* stuck-up.

togs *n coll* clothes; best clothes.

toilet *n* process of dressing, applying cosmetics; **toilet-powder** *n* talcum powder; **toilet-roll** *n* toilet paper; **toilet-table** *n* dressing table.

tokay *n* kind of sweet rich wine from Hungary.

Tom Tiddler's Ground place where money is lying about.

tomfool *adj* extremely foolish.

tommy *n coll* private in the British Army; *sl* bread, provisions.

tomnoddy *n coll* fool.

ton *n* British measure of weight 2,240 lb.

toney *adj* swanky, posh.

tongue, give speak loudly, cry out; support vocally.

ton-up *adj coll* fond of traveling at 100 mph by motorcycle.

too clever by half far too smart; **too true** sadly so.

tool along *coll* drive along smoothly, leisurely; **tool up** equip with machine, electric tools.

tootle *n* telephone call.

top dog person in power, master; **from top to toe** entirely, from head to foot; **top drawer** first class; **top up** add liquid; fill up, esp gasoline; **top it up** fill it; **top-dressing** *n* final coat of paint, varnish; **topflight** *adj coll* first-rate; **top-hole** *adj sl* excellent.

tope *v* drink hard or excessively; **toper** *n* hard-drinker.

topper *n sl* one who or that which is excellent; top-hat.

topping *adj sl* excellent.

torch *n* flashlight.

Tory *n, adj* member of the British Conservative party.

tosspot *n sl* drunkard.

tot *n* tiny child; dram of liquor; *v sl* pick out valuable articles from among refuse.

tottery *adj* unsteady; shaky; tottering.

touch at call at; **touch wood** knock on wood; **touch, put to the** test.

tough *n coll* hooligan, bully; bad luck.

tourer *n* type of open-topped car.

tout round try to pick up tips.

towelling *n sl* thrashing.

towerblock *n* tall apartment house, building.

track, off the the wrong course; **track up** wheel alignment; **trackway** *n* ancient unpaved road.

tradesman *n* storekeeper.

trading-estate *n* area containing houses and light-industry.

trafficker *n* one who deals in illegal trade.

traffic lights stop lights.

t'rah *interj coll* goodbye.

tram *n* streetcar.

transpire *v* exhale as vapor; become known.

transport *n* vehicle, method of conveyance; car; **transport cafe** truckers' stop.

traps *n coll* clothes; belongings.

treacle *n* molasses; **treacly** *adj* syrupy; over-sweet, too affable.

tread *v* walk on; trample; oppress, subdue.

Treasury Bench Parliamentary front bench occupied by chief members of the government.

tree, top of the highest rank, office.

trembly *adj* nervous, inclined to fidget.

trencher *n* cutting-board for meat or bread.

trendy *adj* adopting or popularizing the latest in fashion, idea.

trews *n* tartan trousers.

trice *n* instant, moment.

trick out dress or adorn elaborately.

tricksy *adj* mischievous; deceptive.

trifle *n,* sweet dish of custard, sponge cake, fruit, etc.

trig *n* block to keep a vehicle from rolling; *adj* neat, trim.

trike *n coll* tricycle; three-wheeled car for disabled person.

trilby *n* man's soft felt hat.

trimly *adv* in a trim, neat way.

trimmer *n* opportunist, time-server.

tringle *n* curtain-rod.

tripper *n* one who takes tours or excursions, esp for one day only.

tristful *adj* sad.

trod pt of thread.

troglodyte *n* cave-dweller; recluse.

trolley *n* light, low cart pushed by hand.

trollop *n* immoral and slovenly woman.

trot, on the continually busy; non-stop; **trot out** produce for inspection and approval.

trouble-and-strife *n sl* (cockney) wife.

troublous *adj* agitated, disturbed.

trounce *v* beat; punish; defeat; scold.

trousers *n* pants, slacks; **wear the trousers** wear the pants; woman dominating.

truck *n* open railroad car, esp for coal, wood, etc; two-wheeled luggage cart.

truckle *v* cringe, be servile; **truckle to** submit; **trucklebed** *n* trundlebed.

trug *n* gardening basket of wood-stripping.

trull *n* trollop, strumpet.

trumpery *adj* worthless; rubbish.

trumps, turn up *coll* unexpectedly prove helpful, friendly.

truncheon *n* night-stick.

trunk-call *n* long-distant call; **trunkline** *n* main line of railroad, telephone; **trunkroad** *n* highway, main road joining cities.

try *n* touchdown (rugby).

tub *v coll* take a bath; **tubby** *adj* short and fat; tub-thumper *n* rousing preacher or public speaker.

tube *n* subway; **tube-train** *n* subway train.

tuck *n coll* food, esp cakes, jam and other sweets; **tuckbox** *n* wooden box in which schoolboys keep their tuck; **tuckshop** *n* candy store near a school.

Tudor *adj* of the dynasty that ruled England 1485-1603.

tuffet *n* small, stiffly padded cushion; foot-stool.

tuft-hunter *n* One who seeks company of rich, influential people.

tum *n abbr* tummy, stomach; **tum to** *coll* grasp, hold onto.

tumble to *v* grasp, understand.

tumble-dryer *n* machine dryer.

tumbler *n* glass without a stem.

tump *n* mound.

tun *n* large barrel for wine or beer; 252 gallons.

tundish *n* wooden funnel.

tunny *n* tunafish.

tuppence two pence.

turbot (turbet) *n* large, edible flatfish, similar to flounder.

turf out *coll* dismiss or throw out roughly; **turf-accountant** *n* bookmaker (legal).

turkeycock *n* conceited person.

turkish towelling terry cloth.

turn, done to a perfectly cooked; made; **turn it up** *sl* stop it; shut up; **turn out** *v* drive out; prove to be; become; **turn to** set to work; ask for help from.

turncock *n* water-valve, esp from water-main.

turnpike *n* toll-gate; **turnpike road** toll road.

turn-up *n coll* disturbance, row; **turn-ups** *n* cuffs (pants).

turps *n* turpentine.

tush *interj* exclamation of contempt, disbelief, disapproval.

tusker *n* animal having tusks, large teeth.

tut *interj* exclamation of disapproval, impatience; **tut-tutting** *n, adj* disapproving.

twaddle *n* silly talk, nonsense.

twat *n sl* fool.

twee *adj coll* sweet, pretty-pretty.

tweed *adj, n* Scottish woolen cloth.

tweeny *n coll* servant girl who helps senior maids.

twig *v* grasp; get it; **twiggy** *adj* extremely slim.

twinset *n* sweater-set.

twist, round the crazy; **in a twist** jittery; **don't twist your knickers** don't get upset.

twit *n sl* fool, twerp; **twitty** *adj sl* silly, daft.

twopenny-halfpenny (tupni-haypni) insignificant, petty.

tyre *n* tire.

U

uglify *v* make ugly.

ugly customer dangerous, threatening person.

ugsome *adj* ugly.

Ulsterman *n* native or inhabitant of Northern Ireland.

unbefitting *adj* not suitable to.

unbeknownst *adj* not known.

unbidden *adj* not ordered; spontaneous.

unbosom *v* disclose one's secrets, feelings.

unbrace *v* unfasten; loose, relax.

unbreeched *adj* not yet wearing trousers; still a toddler.

unchancy *adj* bringing bad luck.

unchurch *v* excommunicate.

uncle *n sl* pawnbroker.

unclubbable *adj* unwilling or unable to fit into.

un-come-at-able *adj coll* inaccessible.

uncompanionable *adj* not sociable.

undercarriage *n* landing-gear.

under, down Australia or New Zealand; **under, go** sink, fail; go bankrupt; **under, keep** suppress, hold down.

underground *n* subway.

underlinen *n* underwear.

undraped *adj* naked, nude.

unearth *v* dig up; find something lost or hidden; **unearthly** *adj* absurdly early.

un-English *adj* contrary to English habits, custom, outlook, taste.

unflappable *adj coll* never frighten or upset.

un-get-at-able *adj* inaccessible.

unhandy *adj* not within easy reach; not clever; clumsy.

Union Jack national flag of Great Britain.

unionism *n* policy opposing self-government to territories of the British Empire, esp Ireland.

unit trust mutual fund.

unlettered *adj* not well educated; ignorant.

unlicked *adj* immature; with poor manners.

unlooked-for *adj* uncalled for, unexpected.

unmuzzle *v* allow to speak, roam freely.

unparliamentary language obscene language, swearing.

unperson *n* person whose existence is officially ignored.

unquiet *adj* not quiet, not at peace; anxious, restless.

unrip *v* tear open.

unscholarly *adj* not learned, inaccurate.

unspoilt *adj* not spoiled, undamaged; not over-indulged.

unstick *v* cease to adhere to; come loose.

untoward *adj* inconvenient, regrettable.

unwashed, the great *coll* the mob.

unwifely *adj* unworthy of a wife.

unwinking *adj* with wide-open eyes, vigilant.

up and about on one's feet again; **well up into** expert in; **up, it's all** there's no more hope; **up-country** *adj, n* the interior; ignorant, naive; **upcurrent** *n* trend.

upholster *v* furnish room or house with carpets, curtains, etc.

upmost *adj* uppermost, highest.

upper circle first balcony; **upper dog** the victor; **Upper House** House of Lords; **uppers, on one's** *sl* down and out.

uppish *adj coll* conceited, arrogant; impudent, snobbish.

upshot *n* final result, conclusion.

urchin *n* mischievous small boy.

use, of no useless; **have no use for** *coll* think tedious; dislike.

usher *n* one who walks before a dignitary in a procession.

V

V sign derisive obscene gesture made by forming a V with two fingers, wrist facing outward.

vac *n coll* vacation.

vacancy *n sl* lack of intellect; not all there.

vacant *adj* unoccupied; empty.

vacuum flask thermos bottle.

vainglorious *adj* ostentatiously, boastful.

valet *n* manservant employed to attend to a man's clothes.

valetudinarian *n, adj* person in poor health, or someone overly concerned about one's health.

valorous *adj* exhibiting bravery.

valuer *n* assessor.

valve *n* radio tube.

vamp up patch up to look like new; renovate.

van *n* delivery truck; panel truck.

vandal-proof *adv* unbreakable; wired to discourage thievery.

vanity-bag lady's handbag for cosmetics.

variety *adj theat* vaudeville.

varsity *n coll* university.

vase (vahz) *n* vase.

veg *n coll* vegetable.

velvet, in, on successful; having the advantages.

vent *n* give free expression to.

verdurous *adj* covered with greenery.

verge *n* edge, margin; grass or stone border to a roadway.

verger *n* church caretaker.

vers libre *n Fr* free verse.

very thing exactly what's needed.

Very; Very Light; Very Pistol *n* flare-gun.

vest *n* undershirt; **vest-pocket** *adj* small enough to fit into a vest pocket.

vet; vetted; vetting *v* examine closely and critically; check out.

vex *v* perplex; confuse.

vice *n* vise.

victoria *n* type of light low four-wheeled carriage for two.

Victoria Cross highest British military decoration for valour.

victoriana *n* objects, ideas typical of 19th century.

victualer, licensed innkeeper, one licensed to sell food and drink to be consumed on the premises.

view, on displayed, exhibited.

vinaigrette *n* vinegar container; smelling salts bottle.

vinegary *adj* tasting of vinegar; sour; embittered, spiteful.

vintner *n* liquor store, wine store.

virago *n* shrew; bad-tempered person.

viridescent *adj* greenish.

virtu, vertu *n* object of very rare and exquisitely made.

viscount *n* member of British peerage ranking between earl and baron.

voting-paper *n* ballot.

vulgarian *n* vulgar person, esp one who is also rich.

W

wadding *n* soft fibrous material for quilting, padding.

wafer *n* very thin sweet cookie eaten with ice cream.

waffle *v coll* talk or write too vaguely; talk nonsense.

wage packet pay envelope.

waggery *n* comic remarks or conduct; practical joke.

waggish *adj* comic, droll, mischievous.

waifs and strays homeless persons, esp children.

waistcoat *n* vest.

wakes *n* annual holiday in the North of England.

walk away with win easily; **walk into** *coll* attack, scold, devour; **walk off with** steal; win easily; **walk out with** court, woo.

walkabout *n* royal or important person's informal stroll among crowds.

walkaway *n* easily won contest.

wall box cast iron letter-box built into brickwork.

walla, wallah *n* employee, servant; *coll* an Australian.

wanderplug *n* extension cord.

want *v* lack, lacking, fall short of; be destitute, deficiency.

wanting *adj* needful; insufficient, defective.

warden, traffic traffic policeman.

wardrobe *n* clothes closet; furniture piece for clothing.

warhorse *n* old hand.

warm, British short, thick officer's coat.

warming-pan *n* long-handled metal pan holding live coals, used to warm beds.

wash one's dirty linen in public conduct personal quarrels in presence of others.

wash-house *n* outhouse laundry.

washing powder laundry soap, detergent.

wash-out *n* failure; useless person.

waster *n* spendthrift, ne'er-do-well.

water, in low short of money.

water, of the first of finest quality.

water-biscuit *n* thin, plain hard cracker.

water-closet *n* toilet.

waterwagon, on the *coll* on the wagon, abstaining from alcohol.

waterworks *n coll* urinary system; **turn on the waterworks** *sl* weep.

wattles *n* rods or stakes interwoven with twigs to make fences.

wax *n sl* fit of temper, rage; **waxy** *adj sl* angry

way, give yield; **have a way with one** be charmingly persuasive; **put someone in the way of** give someone an opportunity.

waybill *n* manifest.

way in entrance; **way out** exit.

weakly *adj* poor in health; *adv* in a feeble way.

weald *n* stretch of open country once wooded.

wear *v coll* accept, buy it.

weather, heavy difficulty, trouble; **keep a weather eye open** be on the alert.

weatherboard *n* clapboard.

weathercock *n* windvane, weather-vane.

weather-prophet *n* amateur weather predictor.

weaving, get make an active start, begin energetically.

wedge, thin end of the apparently insignificant event or step that will lead to important results.

weedy *adj* full of weeds; lacking stamina; lanky.

week, this day week from today.

weeny *adj coll* tiny.

weepers *sl* side-whiskers.

weighbridge *n* truck scale.

well away making good progress; *sl* tipsy.

well enough fairly good.

well-connected *adj* from a good, upper-class family.

wellies *n coll* **wellingtons,** waterproof boots.

well-lined *adj* full of money; rich.

wellmeant *adj* said or done with the best of intentions.

wellnigh *adv* very nearly.

well-oiled *adj sl* tipsy; flattering.

Welsh *n, adj* of Wales; Celtic language of Wales; **Welsh dresser** hutch.

West Country Devon and Cornwall, sometimes Somerset.

West End fashionable district of London; the theater district.

Westminster *n* central borough of London; *coll* the government.

wetly *adv* in a wet way.

wetting *n* soaking.

whacked *adj coll* exhausted.

whacker *n sl* anything very large; bold lie.

whacking *n* a thrashing; *adj coll* huge.

whale at expert at; **a whale for** keen on.

what ho *interj* of greeting or surprise.

whatnot *n* shelved cabinet for display of ornaments.

whelk *n* an edible shellfish, like a small conch.

whence comes it that? how is it that?

wherry *n* heavy barge; light rowboat.

whey-faced *adj* sallow, pallid.

whichsoever *pron, adj* whichever.

whiff *n* light, sculling-boat with outriggers.

whilst *prep* while.

whipping-top *n* child's top.

whippy *adj* slender; flexible; nimble.

whisker, within a almost, very nearly; **whiskery** *adj* having long or thick beard.

whiskey *n* Irish whisky.

whisky *n* Scotch whisky.

whist *n* card game for two pairs of players, an early form of Bridge.

white ant termite.

whitebait *n* sprats or young fish eaten as delicacy.

white ensign flag flown by ships of British Navy.

white-headed *adj coll* favorite.

white horses waves with foamy crests.

white lady cocktail of gin and lemon.

white spirit turpentine.

whizzbang *n sl* firework.

whole-hogger *n* enthusiastic, out-and-out supporter.

whopping great *adj* huge.

wick, get on one's annoy, irritate one.

widdershins *adv* counter-clockwise.

wide *adj* far from it; **wide of the mark** just missing.

wigging *n sl* a scolding.

wimple *n* linen veil covering the head and neck.

wind, raise the *sl* raise urgently needed money; **get wind of** hear a hint or rumor of; **put the wind up** *sl* frighten; **sail close to the wind** verge on dishonestly.

windcheater *n* hooded waterproof jacket; windbreaker.

windsail *n naut* wind-chute.

wing *n* fender; (car): *sl* ear.

winking, easy as *coll* very easy; **like winking** *coll* very fast.

winkle *n* an edible shellfish.

winkle-pickers *n coll* shoes with sharp pointed toes.

wireless *n* radio.

wirewool *n* steel wool.

wizard *adj sl* first rate, marvelous.

wodge *n coll* chunk, lump.

wog *n sl* an Arab; an Indian; a Negro; any person of dark color.

wold *n* expanse of open country.

womanish *adj* effeminate, weak.

wonder, I shouldn't *coll* I shouldn't be surprised.

wonky *adj sl* unsteady; wobbly; hesitant; not all right.

won't wash not credible.

woodshed, something nasty in the *sl* shocking secret.

wood-spirit *n* alcohol.

wool, lose one's get angry; **keep your wool on** don't get angry.

woolly *n* sweater.

woolly *adj* made of, covered, resembling wool; *coll* rude, untutored.

worcester sauce worcestershire sauce.

word, have a speak briefly to; **my word!** exclamation of surprise.

wordplay *n* repartee; puns.

workbasket *n* sewing basket.

workshy *adj* unwilling to take a job, lazy.

work-to-rule *n* exaggerated care at work to curtail output.

World, New the Americas; **not for the world** not on any consideration.

world without end eternity.

worship, your mode of address to magistrate.

wotcher *interj sl* what cheer.

wowser *n Aust* puritanical person.

wrangle *v* argue, dispute angrily; **wrangler.**

wrap-up *n coll* elaborate concealment of truth.

wrathy *adj coll* wrathful, angrily.

Wren *n coll* member of Women's Royal Naval Service.

wretched *adj* miserable; dismal, squalid, contemptible, or poor quality.

wriggler *n* one who wriggles, equivocates.

wrong end of the stick misunderstand; get hostile.

Wykhamist *n* past or present pupil of Winchester College.

X

x-legs *n* knock-kneed.

Y

yabber *n, v Aust coll* chatter.
yacht *n* sailboat.
yahoo *n* brutish, bestial person.
yammer *v* yelp, whine; talk nonsense.
yank *n, adj sl* American.
yard, the Scotland Yard.
yard-measure *n* yardstick.
yeasty *adj* frothy; restless; frivolous; wordy.
yellowback *n* cheap sensational novel.
yellow press newspapers unscrupulously sensational.
Yeoman of the Guard bodyguard of the sovereign, now warders or Beefeaters at the Tower of London.
yob *n sl* boy; fellow; lout.
yogs *n sl* ages, years.
Yorkshire on *coll* cheat, swindle, be too smart for.
Yorkshire pudding light batter pudding baked in beef fat.

Z

zebra crossing pedestrian crossing.
zed *n* the letter Z.
zip-fastener *n* zipper.
zounds *interj* mild oath, shorter form of God's wounds.

Common British Abbreviations

A.A.	Automobile Association.
Bart.	Baronet.
Bart's	St. Bartholomew's hosp.
C.B.E.	Commander of the British Empire.
C.E.	Church of England.
C.G.M.	Conspicuous Gallantry Medal.
C.I.	Channel Islands.
C.I.D.	Criminal Investigation Dept.
C.U.	Cambridge University.
D.B.E.	Dame of the British Empire.
D.C.M.	Distinguished Conduct Medal.
D.F.C.	Distinguished Flying Cross.
D.I.Y.	Do-it-Yourself.
D.S.C.	Distinguished Service Cross.
F.B.I.	Federation of British Industries.
F.O.	Flying Officer.
G.P.O.	General Post Office.
G.R.P.	Glass-reinforced plastic; fiberglass.
Hants.	Hampshire.
H.C.	House of Commons.
Herts.	Hertfordshire.
H.H.	His or Her Highness.
H.M.S.	His or Her Majesty's ship.
H.O.	Home Office.
H.R.H.	His or Her Royal Highness.
I.L.O.	International Labour Organization.
I.M.	Isle of Man.
I.R.A.	Irish Republican Army.
I.W.	Isle of Wight.
K.B.E.	Knight of the British Empire.
K.C.	King's counsel.

K.C.B.	Knight Commander of the Bath.
K.G.	Knight of the Garter.
L.	Learner (on cars)
Ltd.	Limited Liability Company.
Leics.	Leicestershire.
Lincs.	Lincolnshire.
Lsd.	Pound, shilling, pence (obsolete).
M.B.E.	Member of the British Empire.
ME	Middle English.
MI5	Intelligence Service.
MI6	Overseas Intelligence.
Mon.	Monmouthshire.
M.O.T.	Inspection for cars.
MP	Member of Parliament.
M.R.	Master of the Rolls.
N.H.S.	National Health Service.
Notts.	Nottinghamshire.
O.B.E.	Order of the British Empire.
O.M.	Order of Merit.
O.U.	Oxford University.
P.A.Y.E.	Pay as you earn.
P.C.	Police constable.
PLC	Public Limited Co.
P.M.	Prime Minister.
Q.C.	Queen's counsel.
R.A.	Royal Academy.
R.A.F.	Royal Air Force.
R.N.	Royal Navy.
Salop	Shropshire.
Staffs.	Staffordshire.
T.U.C.	Trades Union Congress.
U	Upper class; G rating (films).
U.K.	United Kingdom.
V.A.T.	Value Added Tax, tax on non-essential items.

VC	Victoria Cross.
W.C.	Water-closet, toilet.
W.R.A.C., W.R.A.F., W.R.N.S.	Women's Royal Army Corps, Air Force, Naval Service.

Notes

Notes

Notes

Notes

Notes

Notes

Notes

Notes